Tom Richardson
A Bowler Pure and Simple

D1637852

Keith Booth

The most popular cricketer who ever lived was undoubtedly Tom Richardson. He was also the finest fast bowler I have ever seen. I once heard W Lockwood (also a fine fast bowler) say that Richardson was the best fast bowler "ever". And when I remarked to him "What about yourself?" he replied, "I'm not in the same parish."

Herbert Strudwick
Mitcham Cricket Club Yearbook 1937

First published in Great Britain by
Association of Cricket Statisticians and Historians
Cardiff CF11 9XR.
© ACS, 2012

British Library Cataloguing-in-Publication Data.
A catalogue record for this book is available from the British Library.

ISBN: 978 1 908165 19 0
Typeset and printed by The City Press Leeds Ltd

Contents

Foreword by David Richardson   5

Foreword by Martin Bicknell   6

Preface   7

Chapter One   Family Background   8

Chapter Two   Mitcham   13

Chapter Three   1892/94 Surrey... and England   21

Chapter Four   1894/95 Australia   35

Chapter Five   1895... Annus Mirabilis..Surrey   42

Chapter Six   1896... Annus Mirabilis..England   49

Chapter Seven   1897... Jubilee and Millennium   58

Chapter Eight   1897/98 Australia again   64

Chapter Nine   1898/1900 Fin-de-siècle   72

Chapter Ten   1901/12 The Twilight's Last Gleaming   82

Chapter Eleven   Technique and Personality   99

Chapter Twelve   Bout-du-Monde   107

Appendix A   Career Statistics   122

Appendix B   Family Tree   125

Appendix C1   First-Class Cricketers in the
                   Richardson family   126

Appendix C2   ... and their Playing Records   127

Appendix D   Chronology   129

Acknowledgements   132

Bibliography   134

Index   136

Foreword
by David Richardson

Life is full of "what ifs?" and I can't help but reflect on what would have happened to my great-great-uncle Tom, the subject of this fascinating and very welcome biography, if he had followed Frank Richardson, one of his four brothers (and my great-grandfather) and settled in South Africa.

There would not have been the opportunity for Tom to make his living as a professional cricketer but I can well imagine him holding down an honest job in some trade or other during the week and then terrifying local South African players on weekends with his aggressive and accurate no-nonsense fast bowling. If he stood out as exceptional in the county game, who knows what success he may have enjoyed amongst arguably lesser players, in conditions where he could better keep his footing and with a far less taxing workload? With Tom Richardson in its team, perhaps South Africa would not have had to wait until 1906 to achieve its first win in a Test against England.

One thing I do know is that Tom's career was followed with a great deal of pride by his family in South Africa and his success would have been one of the major factors in cementing the interest and enthusiasm for the game amongst the Richardsons in Africa. For that I owe him a huge debt of thanks because it was that interest and enthusiasm which led me to take up the game and, ultimately, to enjoy a life in cricket that has been a joy and a privilege.

The cricket landscape has changed tremendously since the era of Tom Richardson – with coloured clothing, floodlights, Twenty20 cricket, the use of television technology for umpire decision-making and players earning millions of dollars from the game. All these changes are symptomatic of the necessity to move with the times. And yet, it is the history and traditions of cricket that make it special amongst sports. A knowledge of and respect for the former greats, whose feats make up that history, is essential to the game's long-term survival. This book will, no doubt, contribute to such knowledge.

The modern international fast bowler can take comfort from the fact that many of his challenges are little different from those faced by Tom Richardson and his contemporaries – over-bowled, under-appreciated, with a relatively short career span and very little opportunity to enjoy a few pints in the pub without attracting much comment and criticism. Keith Booth's book reminds us that, with more than 2000 first-class wickets, Tom's achievements are worthy of wide recognition and I, for one, will raise a glass to that.

Foreword
by Martin Bicknell

I was very pleased to be asked to write a foreword for Keith Booth's excellent book on Tom Richardson, not least because towards the end of my career, taking a keen interest in the history of Surrey, I found a new hero.

As I crept up the list of Surrey's all-time wicket-takers it always intrigued me to see who was above me, whether I could catch them and where I was going to finish in the list. My last first-class wicket was in 2006 at Bath, on the ground on which Tom finished his first-class career, Andrew Caddick skying a long hop straight up in the air and I finished on 1,026 wickets, placing me fifteenth in the all-time list. Impressive to me, but probably not to Tom Richardson.

Here was a man who knew how to bowl: fast and with incredible stamina, Richardson set the early benchmark for great feats of endurance. In recent times we wrap our bowlers up in cotton-wool, don't over-bowl them and consider 40 overs in a match as a tough game, worthy of the next week off. This man bowled over a hundred overs in a Test Match at Old Trafford, a hundred overs! With pace and accuracy too. Admittedly I wasn't there watching and Sky didn't cover the match but by all reports it was a heroic performance.

And his heroic performances don't end there. Tom went past 100 wickets for the season by 18 June in one year, took 290 wickets in a single season and ended up with just over 2,000 first-class wickets, not bad for a short career. It took me 21 seasons to take just over a thousand!

In that 290-wicket season there were 36 five-wicket hauls and 17 ten-wicket matches too, 61% of the dismissals were bowled which suggests pace, hostility and great accuracy. Career figures aren't too shabby either, 200 five-wicket hauls and 72 ten-wicket matches. Try doing that in modern times.

Tom Richardson is quite an odd selection for a hero of mine, but after you've read the book maybe he'll become one of yours too.

Preface

On the occasion of its hundredth edition in 1963, *Wisden* identified 'Six Giants of the Wisden Century'. They were W.G.Grace, Sir Jack Hobbs, Sir Donald Bradman, Tom Richardson, S.F.Barnes and Victor Trumper. With one exception, all have been the subject of at least one biography and it seemed appropriate to remedy that omission on the centenary of Tom Richardson's premature death.

It is a logical follow-on from my George Lohmann biography, Richardson being Lohmann's heir as Surrey's leading strike-bowler and also a contrast to my previous contribution to the *Lives in Cricket* series, Walter Read. I had in mind at one stage a 'compare and contrast' study – amateur v professional, gentleman v player, but although they overlap slightly, Read's last Test being Richardson's first, they were not quite the same era and it soon became obvious that each merited a biography in his own right.

The subtitle *A Bowler Pure and Simple* is extracted from his *Wisden* obituary and in its context is intended to indicate that neither Richardson nor his contemporaries took his batting and fielding particularly seriously. It is appropriate in a wider context too. As a bowler, he was among the quickest, but he eschewed the 'bouncer' and did not look to intimidate or injure batsmen, just bowl them out. His character off the field reflected that on it. According to his colleagues, he was a genial and sociable man of straightforward tastes – principally a pint or three of ale and an occasional flutter – who related well to his colleagues. Although, like Lohmann he was aware of his professional worth and prepared to drive a hard bargain, 'Honest Tom' was no *prima donna* and even when at the height of his international prestige, threw himself enthusiastically into charitable work and the administrative as well as the playing side of his local club.

The attendance at his funeral reflected the popularity of the man. It was all too soon. His drinking, weight gain and unsuccessful marriage perhaps hastened his demise and provided a pathetic postscript to a purple passage which lasted just four years and for bowling brilliance compares with anything in the history of the game.

Keith Booth
Sutton
June 2012

Note: At various points in this book, sums of money are mentioned. As a rough guide to present day equivalents, the purchasing power of £1 (or 20 shillings) in 1895 was about the same as £90 today.[1]

---

1   *Measuring Worth* website

Chapter One
Family Background

Thomas Richardson was born in a gypsy caravan - or, at least, of Romany stock - in the Surrey town of Byfleet on 11 August 1870. So say a number of sources.[2] Of Byfleet and 11 August 1870 there can be no doubt. His birth certificate confirms that. The gypsy element, however, seems to be a myth, adding a romantic strain to a distinguished career which the great fast bowler himself seems to have made no attempt to deny.

Certainly his looks - black curly hair and ubiquitous Victorian moustache - gave the impression of gypsy ancestry, though there is nothing in his family tree to suggest it. His father was a groom; there is a strong family connection with horses and an Irish strain on his mother's side. Given that gypsies and the Irish were on the margins of the rigid hierarchy of nineteenth-century society, it does not require a doctorate in social anthropology to understand how the myth may have developed. Censuses on which members of the Richardson family appear reveal them as living in houses, not tents or caravans. They seem to have been itinerant and to have moved around in pursuit of work, but it is a *non sequitur* to conclude that they were travellers in the sense implied in Masefield's 'vagrant gipsy life'.

His paternal great-grandfather, who had married Philadelphia Fry (suggesting perhaps a Quaker link, though evidence from the family is that they were Anglican), had ended his days in the Tonbridge Workhouse, and the family connection with horses was not with racehorse ownership or strings of polo ponies, but working with them as grooms and coachmen and mucking out the stables. His grandfather was an agricultural labourer, his father, Henry, a 'Coachman Domestic' in 1871 (Coachman and Domestic Servant on Tom's 1870 birth certificate) and a 'Carman' in 1881, by which time Tom's elder brother Henry was a groom.

His mother was born Johanna Elizabeth Bates, daughter of Irish immigrants Thomas and Catherine Bates, the former born in Woodrough and described as an agricultural labourer on the 1841 Census of Population, simply a labourer ten years later. They were in England by the time Johanna was born in 1837. Both the 1841 and 1851 Censuses find the family living in Putney: Johanna, aged 14 (rounded up to 15) is a 'scholar', so there is an element of education twenty years before state legislation made it compulsory.

---

2   Ralph Barker *Ten Great Bowlers* p 67
Phil Edmonds *100 Greatest Bowlers* p 30
David Frith *The First Great Test Series* p 29
The Fast Men p 61
D.L.A.Jephson *Cricketer* 23 September 1922 p 17
Simon Wilde *The World's Best Batsmen and Bowlers* p 80

Tom Richardson's birth certificate – neither here nor on any other family certificates or censuses is there any reference to or inference of a gypsy caravan or Romany stock.

Tom was the fourth of seven children with three elder brothers and two younger sisters, the second one twinned with the youngest brother; his father had seven siblings, his mother four, so there was a plethora of aunts, uncles and cousins. There would not have been much money around on either side of the family and existence was probably not very much above the breadline. So, like many fast bowlers, the origins are firmly working class, at the base of the pyramid of Victorian society. In his childhood, the family moved from Byfleet to Mitcham where he spent his formative teenage years.

All the family were present at 8 Hancock's Cottages on Commonside East on Census Night in 1881 along with a lodger employed at the brickworks, but ten years later, the three elder brothers, Harry, Bill and Frank had left home (Frank was a groom with the Queen's Royal West Surrey Regiment in India), Tom, now described as a 'Professional Cricketer', was still living there, as was Charlie, now aged 16 and a butcher, and sister Ellen, aged 19, a domestic servant. Charlie's twin sister, Alice, was not there, possibly in residential domestic service elsewhere. It was a common occupation for teenage girls at the time.

Their mother died aged 54, in Croydon General Hospital in 1891, of diabetes, a growth in the bladder, haemorrhage and debility - a year before Tom made his Surrey début. He was with her at her death.

Tom married Edith Emma Cheesman, in 1895. She was twenty-one at the time and the daughter of Charles Cheesman and Emma Hampton. Her father, who had died in 1887, was a leather dresser in 1871, a skinner

9

*Hancock's Cottages on the fringe of Mitcham Common
where Tom grew up with his six siblings.*

in 1881; one of her elder brothers was a leather dresser, her mother a charwoman, her aunts, grandmother and great-grandmother laundresses. By 1891, Emma had moved out from her widowed mother's home and was working as an assistant for her septuagenarian paternal grandfather at the Queen's Head at Beddington Corner. Given Tom's known propensity for a pint of ale (or more), it seems at least likely that this was where the couple met. On the occasion of the marriage in 1895, the Surrey Club presented Tom with £20[3] and the ball with which he had taken four wickets in an over.

Ten years earlier, Mr and Mrs Walter Read had benefited by £250 and a clock. The difference epitomised the way in which Surrey and other counties treated their amateur and professional cricketers.

The couple had three children, Kathleen, Tom and Edith, born at two-year intervals from 1898 to 1902, the first two (Edith was yet to be born) living with their parents in Thames Ditton in 1901. There was something of an extended family there as included in the Census return are Tom's younger sister, Alice and Edith's Aunt Hannah.

Charles Alcock suggests that Richardson was born in Mitcham and that several generations of his ancestors hailed from there:

> Mitcham has in its time furnished many distinguished cricketers to the Surrey eleven. The latest is Richardson, whose forebears have been closely associated with the little village which gave the Humphreys and Jones among latter day players to County cricket.[4]

As a professional journalist, Alcock was normally more meticulous about checking his sources, but this was in what today would be styled a coffee-table book where historical accuracy is sacrificed to presentation and pretty pictures. Facts, however, should not be allowed to spoil a good story and they have become clouded by a layer or two of mythology.

Tom's elder brother Bill, the second eldest, spent the remainder of his days in Mitcham, plying his trade as a boot-maker and dying there in 1948. A few years before that he was profiled in the local newspaper:

> Bill Richardson is old Mitcham in everything but birth. He is a Cockney according to the Registers and if Finsbury[5] is within the sound of Bow Bells. His father was a horse doctor[6] (the old fashioned substitute for a 'vet') in Ropemaker Street in the City and came to Mitcham when Bill was ten to manage a branch business for his employers in Lewis Road. Tom Richardson, four years younger than Bill was born in Byfleet so it will be seen that the Richardson family was not static at that time.
>
> "All we Richardsons learnt our cricket on Mitcham Green and we began young. Tom was a genius at the game from the start. He was soon spotted by Tom Harvey and other big fry and yanked off to play with

---

3   Surrey CCC minutes 17 October 1895
4   *Famous Cricketers and Cricket Grounds*
5   An error repeated in his obituary: censuses say 'Dorking'. Charles was born in Finsbury.
6   Maybe an exaggeration. Censuses say 'Carman', 'Coachman' and 'Coal dealer'.

teams as old again as himself and with years more experience. He was as strong as I was weak. Infantile paralysis was my undoing, at two years of age, yet at ten I was playing cricket on the Green and my subsequent career with the 'Old Buffers', a good old all-Mitcham team of repute, showed that I did not allow my disability to handicap me unduly. Like Tom I was a bowler, but, unlike him, a slow one. It was my pride that I could make the ball turn either way."

Bill Richardson had a proper pride in his famous brother:

"Tom took his first wicket in first-class cricket at the Oval with the first ball he sent down," he said.[7] "The first victim was Burns, the Essex professional. Some years after my brother Charles, bowling his first ball as professional for Upminster Friars took the wicket of Burns's brother. Strange things happen in cricket and I think that is one of the strangest."[8]

The youngest brother, Charles (actually Launcelot Charles, but none of the five brothers was known by their first given name),[9] referred to here, played for Mitcham Wanderers in at least one match against F.G. Owers, part of the family who accompanied Tom to Aix-les-Bains on what turned out to be his final holiday.

The third brother, Francis (Frank) followed a military career as a groom. He joined the Queen's Royal West Surrey Regiment in 1888; army records indicate that he had previously been a groom with the 5th Battalion of the Royal Fusiliers. He served in India, South Africa in the Boer War, Canada and South Africa again where the family settled. He is the great-grandfather of former South African wicket-keeper, now General Manager - Cricket of the ICC, David Richardson. There are several other first-class cricketers among the descendants of Tom's siblings, as well as an international hockey player[10] and an Olympic yachtsman.[11] The whole family has an impressive sporting pedigree with several examples of provincial representation, and current members recall the previous generation playing against Bob Willis in club cricket in Pretoria.

Tom predeceased all of them. Bill and Charles were the chief mourners at his funeral: Harry does not get a mention.[12] Frank was in South Africa.

---

7   The recollection is correct, but Essex was not first-class at the time.

8   *Mitcham Advertiser* 20 August 1942.

9   Charles Henry was known as Harry, William as Bill, Francis as Frank, Thomas as Tom and finally, Launcelot Charles as Charles.

10   Margaret Cowen (née Richardson) , Frank's granddaughter represented South Africa in the 1960s.

11   Ian Ainslie who represented South Africa in the Olympic Games in 1992, 1996 and 2000.

12   *Mitcham Advertiser* 19 July 1912

Chapter Two

Mitcham

The family home where Tom spent his formative years was 8 Hancock's Cottages, one of a row of eleven on Mitcham's Commonside East. Some of the cottages were demolished and rebuilt as Alston Cottages in 1906 and have now been renumbered with Commonside East addresses. A stone's throw away is the Three Kings public house and the Three Kings pond which coaches used to recontract the expanding metal and re-expand the contracting wood of their wheels. Literally across the road from Hancock's Cottages is the northern tip of the vast expanse of Mitcham Common, flat and grassy here, an ideal play area for children provided they didn't go too close to the pond, while further north, the terrain becomes steeper and overgrown with bracken and other dense shrubbery.

The Richardsons' neighbours included a gardener, a carpenter, a factory labourer, a painter's labourer, gasworks labourer, dressmakers and laundresses, so the area was respectable, solid working-class: no evidence here of gypsy blood. Those who had that flowing through their veins were across the road on the Common.

The 1881 Census of Population reveals a number of gypsies living in tents and caravans whose professions are described as hawkers, pegmakers and general dealers. It is likely that the Richardson children would have played with the Romany children and this social interaction may well have led to the unsubstantiated rumour that the family had gypsy blood.

Gypsies continued to live on Mitcham Common well into the twentieth century and were regular visitors to Mitcham Fair, held every August, not very long after the Derby meeting on nearby Epsom Downs. In between the travellers would look for work picking the local lavender and some settled in an area known colloquially by the locals as 'Redskin Village' because of the number of tents pitched there. According to the late Ralph Barker,[13] the Richardson family also lived in Redskin Village, but the evidence is against this. They appear on successive censuses as resident at Hancock's Cottages and Redskin Village was, according to local historian Eric Montague, near Phipps Bridge, some way to the west of the Common. Nor does there seem to be any support for Barker's statement that Richardson lived in a 'slum cottage'. The 1881 Census of Population would not have been available to him when he was writing in the mid-1960s, but Hancock's Cottages[14] seem to be home to respectable, if not affluent, artisans.

---

13 *Ten Great Bowlers* p 97
14 There is a local legend that the Cottages are haunted, the *Mitcham News and Mercury* reporting in February 1962 that images of cavaliers, grenadiers, women and young children had appeared on the walls during replastering. The cottages are very close to Rose Cottage which is also alleged to be haunted.

Mitcham Green: the first mention of cricket being played there is 1685.

Montague draws the background of Mitcham, cricket and gypsies:

> The mid-Victorian period was recalled with obvious nostalgia by a
> number of old Mitcham residents who recorded their memories in the
> 1920s. Cricket was the great game, played on the Lower Green by all
> classes. Mitcham vied with Hambledon for the distinction of being the
> cradle of club cricket in the 18th century, and by the 1830s and '40s
> could field a team fit to take on all comers. The annual fair, held on 12,
> 13 and 14 August on the Upper Green,[15] was regarded as an event of
> considerable antiquity and looked forward to by many.
>
> Gypsies, attracted by the fair and the prospect of employment in
> the herb gardens came to Mitcham in droves after the Epsom races.
> Dozens of their colourful caravans and tents could often be seen
> on the Common, where they made their own entertainment with
> impromptu horse racing and bare knuckle fights. Many were to settle
> in Mitcham, finding permanent sites for their vans in the yards off
> Western Road, and in the neighbourhood of Phipps Bridge, nicknamed
> 'Redskin Village'.[16]

At times, some of the gypsy population operated at the margins of legality,
as when one of their number was found guilty by local magistrates of
acting as a pedlar without a licence and obtaining threepence by fraud and
false pretences.[17]

Tom was educated at the 'National School for the Education of the Poor
according to the Principles of the Church of England', located close to the
Lower Green. Because of increasing numbers of children, especially after

---

15   The customary site of the fair until 1924 when it was relocated on the 'Three
      Kings' Piece'

16   *Mitcham - A Pictorial History* - pages are unnumbered.

17   *Wimbledon Times* 17 August 1889

the Education Act of 1870 which made elementary education compulsory, the school was extended periodically, but was the subject of several reports which condemned it as insanitary. It closed in 1898. On leaving school, Tom found a job as a labourer in a linoleum factory on Morden Road.

It was not a job he enjoyed and he applied to join the Army and the Police Force but was rejected by both, allegedly because of a heart abnormality[18] which his later feats of stamina seemed to belie. It is at least possible that he wished to follow his brother's example and join the Queen's Royal West Surrey Regiment.[19] Had he done so, the history of fast bowling might have been different.

Anecdotal evidence from the family is that by the end of the century Tom had made sufficient money from professional cricket to enable him to buy a few of the cottages and rent them out. The only member of the family remaining there in 1901 was eldest brother Charles Henry (known as Harry), who is described as an insurance agent and may possibly have been acting as a letting agent for Tom.

Mitcham Cricket Club is one of a number which claims to be the oldest in the world, difficult to prove as the informal playing of the game generally precedes the formal establishment of a cricket club, but *Crickette on Ye Olde Meecham Green* is reputed to have been shown in a print dated 1685[20] and there is substance in the boast that the Green is the ground with the longest record of continuous use. Whatever its origins, in the early nineteenth century it was clearly well established:

> At Mitcham a club of noblemen and gentlemen amuse themselves three or four times a week, and most of them are good hands.[21]

The Richardsons were by no stretch of the imagination 'noblemen and gentlemen' and by the time they arrived in Mitcham the Club had become more representative of the population of the village. Over the years it has been a regular and prolific nursery for the county, producing early Surrey 'crack' James Southerton, Herbert Strudwick, and in more recent times, Ken Barrington. In the late nineteenth century, the Club regularly hosted practice facilities for the Australian tourists. By 2012 Mitcham Cricket Club had slipped to the sixth tier of the Surrey Championship, but it remains proud of its heritage and traditions.

> Scores of times I have been asked where I learnt my cricket and have been very pleased to say, "At Mitcham" and my questioner has said, "Oh, yes, the nursery of Surrey cricket". I recall hearing people suggest that one end of the wicket was dry and the other wet, one for Tom Richardson and the other one for T.P.Harvey! I never saw such a thing and think the suggestion was just somebody's imagination. T.P.Harvey was a slow right-arm bowler with a slight suspicion of a throw. He

18   Barker *Ten Great Bowlers* pp 68 & 125 ; the Richardson family has a history of congenital heart disease.

19   Recruitment records for the period are no longer extant.

20   Website of Merton Historical Society

21   *Annals of Sporting* June 1822

could make the ball turn on any wicket. So with Tom Richardson at one end and two slow bowlers like T.P.Harvey[22] and J.Keene[23] at the other it might have appeared so. These three were a great combination. Most of the matches in those days were whole day affairs, and the Club headquarters was at the "Cricketers", then kept by J.Southerton, who served a fine lunch.[24]

Two other teams played on the Green at the time at this time. The "Old Buffers" [sic] in front of the police station and Mitcham Wanderers opposite the Vestry Hall. Each of them were responsible for bringing many youngsters to the front. The Wanderers, at one time, had five men in the side who played in county cricket, R.Pearson, E.Bale, R.Turner (Worcester), Dan Sullivan (Surrey and Glamorgan) and myself.[25]

That was Herbert Strudwick, reminiscing in the 1930s. The 1938 Yearbook mentions twenty Mitcham-born cricketers who had played for the Surrey county 1st XI – and that excludes Southerton and Richardson who were born elsewhere. He goes on to mention Tom's brother, Charlie, as a member of the Wanderers team. The young Tom Richardson learned his cricket in the same nursery and made an immediate impact. His first match was for the 'Old Buffer's' Cricket Club, Mitcham's junior wing. Organised by Fred Gale, they played on another part of the Green, opposite their headquarters, the Britannia public house, and took their name from the pseudonym under which Gale wrote in *Bailey's Magazine*. It was not long, however, before the young fast bowler graduated to the senior side.

In the 1890s it was quite usual for there to be three matches in progress simultaneously:[26] Mitcham and the 'Old Buffer's' and the parallel side of Mitcham Wanderers which Strudwick represented before achieving greater distinction on the county and international stages.

At the turn of the century the ground was unfenced and there was no pavilion. Tents were erected for changing facilities. That was all to change in 1904 when the still used pavilion was first opened, the occasion being marked by a match between the Mitcham Club and a county eleven raised by Richardson. The road which separates the pavilion from the playing area is now rather busier than it was at the time and adds an interesting dimension to present-day cricket on Mitcham Green which in 1969 was recognised as a Conservation Area by the London Borough of Merton.

In 1889, Tom appears in the Mitcham team photograph, so it is to be assumed that he was playing regularly for them. On 20 May 1890 he played

---

22 Thomas Harvey (b 1860) never played first-class cricket, but played for Gentlemen of Surrey (1887 -1889), Surrey 2nd XI (1891-98) and Surrey Club and Ground (1893)

23 John Keene later played for Surrey, Worcestershire and Scotland.

24 James Southerton had died in 1880, the same year in which Strudwick was born when Richardson was a boy of nine. His widow, Sarah, continued to run the 'Cricketers', so the J.Southerton referred to here is clearly one of the Southerton family rather than the famous 19th century professional cricketer.

25 *Mitcham Cricket Club Yearbook* 1937: Pearson and Bale did not play first-class cricket; Richard Turner played 52 matches for Worcestershire either side of the First World War and Dennis Sullivan 132 matches for Surrey and Glamorgan between 1914 and 1928.

26 Francis *Old Mitcham* - pages are unnumbered

Ball Games are now prohibited.

Mitcham Cricket Club now.

for Mitcham against Surrey Club and Ground, but took no wickets, then the following week, probably[27] for Mitcham again against Surrey Colts and had three for 39.

Such coaching as he had came from Arthur Woodcock, himself a fast bowler, later to distinguish himself with Leicestershire, who was associated with Mitcham in the late 1880s and reported to a local journalist that, at this development stage of Richardson's career, he preferred six hours of hard work in the nets to an hour's ordinary work elsewhere.[28] The stamina he developed and the appetite for hard work were to remain with him throughout most of his career.

In 1891, the year he reached his twenty-first birthday, Tom took 102 wickets at 7 each and contributed to an outstanding season for his club in which they won twenty and drew nine of thirty matches played. One of their more significant victories was against Surrey Club and Ground. Richardson played for Mitcham and took five wickets in the first innings and six in the second. No analysis is given, but it must have been a satisfactory victory for Mitcham - by an innings and 3 runs. In the same season, playing this time for, rather than against, the Club and Ground, against Fourteen Colts he had 18-9-20-8 and 9-3-10-2.[29]

In his *Chats on the Cricket Field*,[30] W.A.Bettesworth ascribes the following anecdote to O.R.Borradaile, Secretary of Essex. It is not absolutely certain that it relates to Richardson, but the likelihood is that it does – and it's a good story anyway:

> In April 1902 Mr Borradaile attended the dinner of the Stoics CC of which he was honorary secretary for many years and was then captain. In the course of the evening he told the following story. "It was in a match down Mitcham way," he said, "and the bowler – I think it was Richardson – pitched a very fast ball right on the batsman's instep, and appealed for leg-before-wicket. Without a shadow of doubt the man was plumb in front, and the umpire unhesitatingly gave him out. But he took no notice of the decision, and still went on rubbing his instep. Presently the wicket-keeper … said 'I'm afraid, Sir, you'll have to go. The umpire has given you out leg-before-wicket!' To which the batsman gave the unexpected reply, 'That's all right, I'm going as soon as ever as I can move."

Tom had been on the Surrey staff from 1890.[31] It was two years later that he first played for the First XI, but he was appearing regularly for the Colts and made occasional appearances for the Second Eleven, including one against Fifteen of Dorking and another against Fifteen of Guildford, but without success.[32] His entry in the Census of Population for the following

---

27   The *Surrey Yearbook* says 'J' Richardson, probably a misprint. It may have been one of his brothers, though none of them was 'J'.

28   *Richmond Herald*   6 July 1912

29   *Surrey Yearbook* 1892

30   p 68. It appeared originally in the *Cricket Field* on 25 August 1894

31   Tom Higgs, Mitcham Cricket Club historian. *Mitcham Cricket Club Yearbook* 1989

32   *Surrey Yearbook* 1890

year confirms that he is now a professional cricketer.

Such local newspaper evidence as there is confirms Bill Richardson's later recollection that all the Richardsons played cricket on the Green with one or other of the three Mitcham sides. Against Mr J.W.Hobbs' Club on 30 August 1890, Frank had three wickets.[33] He was on the card at No 11, so batting was clearly not a Richardson family strong point.

Tom's performances for Mitcham and obvious potential earned him three inter-county matches with the Surrey Second Eleven in 1891, two against Bedfordshire and one against Nottinghamshire. Ten wickets at under twelve, including 7-3-10-4 at Luton, was sufficient to keep him in the frame. He also played a few matches for a successful Club and Ground Eleven which lost only one of its 27 matches – to Mitcham.

In his early days, Tom would have earned something like 30 to 38 shillings per week, not a lot, but as for most professionals, it was pay for something he enjoyed doing and certainly more than he was earning in the linoleum factory. Agricultural labourers were paid about half of what he received as a junior professional. His pay as an unskilled worker would not have been much more.[34]

His attachment to Mitcham continued until his marriage and move to Thames Ditton in 1895 and, when not required by Surrey or when the county had no fixture or had finished a three day match in two, he would turn out for the club. In 1892 he took five wickets – all bowled - against Whitgift Wanderers[35] and in 1893, five against Croydon and six against Thames Ditton.[36] Full bowling figures were rarely given in the press for club and school matches.

Mitcham Cricket Club in 1889: Richardson extreme right on front row.
[Mitcham Cricket Club]

---

33   *Cricket* 11 September 1890
34   W Robson *Twentieth Century Britain* p 165
35   *Croydon Chronicle* 16 July 1892
36   *Cricket*   11 May and 22 June 1893

Back Row:

D. KNAPP. Umpire.

A. WOODCOCK. Fast bowler and groundsman. At one time engaged by Leicester County C.C.

G. SPILLMAN. Good bat and wicket keeper. Kept wicket for Middlesex County C.C.

T. RICHARDSON. The incomparable. Mitcham, Surrey, England.

H. LIDDEN. A fine all rounder. On ground staff at Oval.

W. W. THOMSON. An official of the Club for many years.

Front Row.

J. CAFFREY. Splendid bat. Also played for J. W. Hobbs' XI—famous team of the period.

N. A. HARVEY. A great all rounder.

T. P. HARVEY. The greatest Mitcham skipper in living memory. Bat, bowl and field superbly. Skippered Surrey Second XI. County Hockey player

F. HARRIS. Left arm bowler and fine field.

A. F. CLARKE. Renowned wicket keeper. Kept for Surrey.

In Front.

J. BOXALL. Fine bat and bowler. On Oval ground staff and played for County. Later groundsman on Green.

H. PILLINGER. Splendid bat. Several tours with Surrey C. & G.

Mitcham Cricket Club in 1891.
[Mitcham Cricket Club]

Chapter Three
1892-94 Surrey...and England

1892

RICHARDSON, the young cricketer who came to the fore this season as a fast bowler, it will be of interest to the followers of Surrey cricket to know, is a native of the County, as I pointed out some thirteen months ago. Though born at Byfleet, Mitcham can fairly claim the credit of his education, as he has lived the best part of his life and played his cricket there. He was twenty-two years of age in July last.[37]

Residence in a county was significant as a qualification, though Surrey had a reputation for recruiting from outside the county and George Lohmann, Tom Bowley, John Sharpe, John Beaumont and Bill Lockwood can be numbered among those who were not Surrey-born.

Before he became established on the national cricket scene, Richardson added to his income by doing a bit of net bowling at Winchester College. More than fifty years later, Sir Henry Leveson Gower remembered the impression he made:

> ... our cricket master managed to get a bowler of pace for us who a few years later became very famous.[38] This was Tom Richardson of Surrey. Here was a splendid specimen of a young trier who would never bowl to hurt you but was always eager to bowl to give you practice for any particular stroke that you wished to learn. He had a splendid action, and his appearance was such that anyone looking at him would feel impelled to say: "Surely that man is a cricketer!"[39]

He fulfilled a similar rôle at Cambridge University where he played a part in helping Ranjitsinhji acclimatise to English conditions. Ranji's near contemporary, Digby Jephson, later to captain Surrey, has the following anecdote about an early season visit to the nets at Fenner's:

> One day twelve years ago, early in April, I strolled into Fenner's thinking that a little practice might be of service to me. I am but a poor bat today, then I was infinitely worse. I journeyed to the nets (as most people know they are not of the best) with the usual equipment of pads and gloves. Out from the pavilion came a thin, lithe form of a man, with black curly hair. I took the usual guard; he took a run of some seven yards. I believe the ball pitched six inches outside the off

---

37   *Cricket* 1 September 1892: His birthday was actually August
38   This was to help the Winchester batsmen deal with Dudley Forbes, Eton's fast bowler who went on to play for Oxford University. He died of enteric fever in South Africa in 1901, aged 28. The master in charge of cricket was former Oxford University and Middlesex cricketer, E.H.Buckland.
39   *Off and On the Field* p 37

stump, at any rate it came back like lightning and the middle stump disappeared into the net; the next ball, pitching nearly straight, hit me on the chest; the third removed the off stump; the fourth hit me on the arm; the fifth removed the leg stick; the sixth and seventh found my ribs.

I said "Thank you very much, I don't think I'll practise any more today," and walking away painfully back to the "hutch" I thought in future I would take a breastplate instead of a bat – it might be of more use; it certainly could not be of less.

"Who was that bowling?" I asked.

"Oh a young fellow named Richardson – Surrey, I think," was the answer.

I had never seen such bowling.[40]

Fast bowlers hunt in pairs. With Larwood and Voce, Trueman and Statham, Lillee and Thomson, Ambrose and Walsh, there could be no escape at 'the other end'. It was no different when Richardson joined Surrey. Five years earlier *Cricket* had reported with enthusiasm:

W.LOCKWOOD, the young professional who made his *début* for Notts against Gloucestershire at Moreton-in-the-Marsh (sic) at the end of June, and bowled in very promising form against the Australians last week, seems likely, as far as one can judge from his earliest efforts to be of no small use to the County. He was born in Radford, near Nottingham, and will not be nineteen years of age till next March. He learned his cricket in Nottingham Forest, and first came into notice last year in a series of matches played by the Forest Cricket Association. He bowls round arm[41] with a high delivery and though inclined to be short, gets up very quickly from the pitch.[42]

The Editor of *Cricket* happened to be the Secretary of Surrey County Cricket Club on whose books the young Nottinghamshire professional found himself three years later. The county were fortunate, maybe even prescient, in having recruited Bill Lockwood, one of several bowlers who partnered George Lohmann before the latter's decline in health compelled him to abandon Surrey for two seasons. The way was thus clear for Lockwood and Richardson to team up and keep Surrey at the forefront of county cricket for most of the 1890s.

In the wake of Tom's successful performances with the Second XI and Club and Ground XI, a First XI début against Essex (not first-class at the time) at The Oval followed in May 1892, when the absence of Abel, Lohmann, Sharpe and Maurice Read playing in Alfred Shaw's benefit match and the unavailability of W.W.Read, provided an opportunity of which the young fast bowler took full advantage:

---

40   *Surrey Cricket: its History and Associations* pp 225-226
41   ie overarm: 'round arm' was frequently used at the time to distinguish it from 'underarm' which, though less fashionable than formerly, remained legal for a further century.
42   15 July 1886

Cricket on the Lower Green, Mitcham, 1895.
[London Borough of Merton Local Studies Library]

… no one made any stand against Richardson's bowling and the match ended soon after five o'clock on Tuesday in an easy win for Surrey by 195 runs. Richardson who was born and has lived all his life in Mitcham[43] made a very successful *debut* for Surrey. He is a fast right handed bowler with a high delivery. He gets up quickly off the pitch and as he comes back at times a good deal he bids fair to be of use.[44]

His figures of 17-7-45-6 and 19.3-5-55-6 compare more than favourably with those of Essex speed merchant Charles Kortright's 8-1-26-3 and 14.2-5-45-2 and he turned out to be rather more than 'of use'.

A first-class début against Cambridge University produced an undistinguished one for 94 across the two innings in a match which Surrey lost by 80 runs. Before the end of June, however, Tom had made his presence felt with 30-8-67-7 and 30.1-6-63-5 in another non-first-class fixture at Derby.

> Richardson's bowling was quite one of the best features of the match. Altogether he took twelve Derbyshire wickets for less than eleven runs a-piece. Chatterton received a blow on the head from a ball of Richardson, and had to retire when he had made sixteen, though he was able to finish his innings.[45]

On his Championship début against Gloucestershire he had five for 43 in the second innings, the first of 200 'five-for's in a distinguished career,

---

43   Not so – see Chapter One
44   *Cricket* 19 May 1892
45   *Cricket* 23 June 1892

in a match which Surrey won by eight wickets.[46] The report in *Cricket is* silent on Richardson's bowling, preferring to concentrate on the fact that W.G.Grace allowed Watts to act as substitute wicket-keeper for Clarke. In the same match George Lohmann took his 1500th first-class wicket. It may not have been realised at the time, but the torch was passing on. In another age, Richardson might have been Man of the Match, though Lockwood with five first-innings wickets would also have a strong claim, as would Maurice Read or Henderson for their batting. It was a good start. Ten more first-class matches followed that season, his final tally being 29 wickets at just over 20. He had joined a successful side. Over six seasons, Surrey had won three out of every four of their first-class county matches and carried off the County Championship for the third consecutive season.

In other matches he filled his boots – 12 wickets in a match against Lancashire Second XI, 15 against Essex, 11 against Leicestershire – plus the odd five-wicket innings in between - a portent of things to come.

There is a local myth that Richardson walked from Mitcham to The Oval on home match days. There is no evidence one way or the other. It is known from interviews with his son that he was fond of walking long distances and doubtless this habit contributed to his fitness. It would not be out of character for him to do so, but, except possibly in his early days as a junior pro, it is unlikely that he did. Tom Higgs, historian of Mitcham Cricket Club, has looked at Richardson's financial position, based on evidence unearthed by Ric Sissons, and concluded that, once established in the county side, he could well afford to take public transport in the form of the horse bus.

1893

Great Drought of 1893

THE drought of 1893 will unquestionably take its place among the recorded events of history, if regard be had to its intensity, the length of time during which it has lasted, and the wide extent of the earth's surface it has overspread. Treating the British Islands as a whole, the drought may be considered as embracing by much the greater part of the country for the fifteen weeks beginning with March 5. But while copious rains have fallen during the past few weeks in many places, it may be regarded as continued to near the present time in many of the more important agricultural districts in the south.[47]

Whatever the disadvantages to agriculture, the meteorological conditions of 1893 provided the kind of hard, fast pitches on which Tom Richardson was to excel. Almost literally he hit the ground running and Albert Craig, the Surrey poet, had no doubt about the apostolic succession:

When George Lohmann sail'd away
To a foreign shore
Surrey griev'd but yearned to see,

---

46   *Cricket* 30 June 1892
47   *Nature* 27 July 1893

See his face once more.
Tom now takes our champion's place,
Stands beside his gun;
Yes, George Lohmann's mantle fell,
Fell on Richardson.

Neither had *Wisden:*

> The chief cause of the falling off of the county is revealed at once by a glance at the averages. Lohmann's illness and consequent inability to play made, of course, an enormous difference, but the loss of his bowling was compensated for to a far greater extent than could possibly have been expected by the development of Richardson, and it was the decline in the batting, not in the bowling, that brought the eleven down from their high estate.[48]

Richardson provided the consistency which Lockwood lacked and, despite a damaged finger which prevented his playing a few matches in late June and early July, he could eventually look back with satisfaction on a season which not only saw him become an automatic choice for Surrey when fit, but also one which led to representative cricket and a Test début.

Although in 1893, Surrey, without Lohmann, fell slightly from grace, slipping to fifth place in the Championship and conceding the title to Yorkshire, this was the first season in which Richardson made a massive impact on the county scene. Outside the Championship Derbyshire never recovered from his 28-12-36-8 in the first innings. Of his twelve wickets in the match, ten were bowled. A similar ratio was to characterise his bowling throughout his career.

> Mr Wright and Chatterton alone withstood the bowling of Richardson...

This was also an occasion on which he made an impact with the bat:

> ... the best feature of the latter part of the innings was the free hitting of the last two batsmen, who knocked up 64 for the last wicket.[49]

Batting at No.11, as he usually did, Richardson had 34 of them.

At Trent Bridge, in his first first-class appearance of the season, in the traditional Whitsuntide fixture, seven wickets in the first innings ensured that a strong Nottinghamshire, the county which had dominated the scene in the preceding three decades, were never in the match. They were obliged to follow on and a further seven scalps in the second innings paved the way to a seven wicket victory.

> To Richardson's fast bowling was due the cheap dismissal of a strong batting side. Seven of the wickets fell to him at an average of under nine runs. As they were 121 runs behind Notts had to follow on. Richardson again took seven wickets at a cost of twelve runs apiece. In the match altogether he took fourteen wickets at an aggregate cost of 145 runs.[50]

---

48   1894 p 78
49   *Cricket* 25 May 1893
50   *Cricket* 25 May 1893

Groundsman Walker ruefully survived the wreckage:

> two tons of water have I put on it, but had I been told about that young
> fast bowler from Surrey, I fancy I would have given it another ten. [51]

It was in this match that accusations of throwing first emerged. ICC's
fifteen-degree regulation was more than a century away and at a time
when the distinction between bowling and throwing and the relative roles
of the wrist and the elbow in the bowling action were less well defined,
Richardson was one of several bowlers whose actions were deemed to
be suspect and led two years later to the establishment of a Doubtful
Delivery Sub-Committee. Among suspects were Arthur Mold of Lancashire
and C.B.Fry. Earlier there had been John Crossland and George Nash, also
of Lancashire and later, the Australian, Ernest Jones. Rev R.S.Holmes,
however, had few doubts.

> If I were selecting the team to do battle for England just now, Flowers and
> Richardson would have to be reckoned with. Mention should be made
> of sundry adverse comments passed at Trent Bridge on Richardson's
> delivery especially when he sent down his fast yorker. "A throw," said
> the Notts cricketers; a throw said most of the representatives of the
> Fourth Estate. "What is a throw?" asked I of one of them in return
> and not one of them could give me any satisfactory answer. I watched
> the Surrey bowler with a terrier-like scrutiny and Richard Daft did the
> same. Would it be credited that neither of us suspected his delivery
> before hearing this outcry, and that subsequently we could discover
> no grounds for the charge? I feel it to be my duty most emphatically
> to protest against this clamour; is it fair to a young bowler thus to
> affix a black mark to him? If anyone can throw and keep a stiff elbow
> then bowling may be throwing and *vice versa;* but a throw is quite
> impossible by any movement of the wrist alone and Richardson simply
> gives a flick of the wrist when he puts down his express. [52]

Neither the Nottinghamshire batsmen nor *Wisden* were as convinced:

> The victory was brought about by the amazingly effective fast bowling
> of Richardson, who took in all fourteen wickets for 145 runs. This was
> an extraordinary performance, but we are bound to add that several
> of the Notts players – not, we think, without good reason – questioned
> the fairness of the very fast ball with which he obtained most of his
> wickets. [53]

and again:

> Into the question of his delivery we do not feel called upon to enter
> at any great length. We are certainly of opinion that the Notts players
> had ample reason to take exception to the fairness of his very fast ball
> in the match at Trent Bridge on Whit Monday, and we happen to know
> that, though he escaped no-balling, one of the umpires was strongly
> of opinion that on occasion he threw. In subsequent matches, when

---

51   *Cricket*   1 June 1893
52   *Cricket*   1 June 1893
53   1894 p 109

we saw him, his delivery was far less open to objection, and, though an occasional ball looked like a throw, we quite believe that he did his best to be strictly fair. Leaving the dispute as to his delivery aside, he clearly proved himself an extraordinary bowler.[54]

It was not in Richardson's character to cheat deliberately. He was a natural, received little coaching and at this early stage of his career had not 'honed' his action. There is no subsequent record of suspicion though, so it must be assumed that whatever flaws existed were quickly and easily ironed out.

Eleven wickets against the touring Australians followed as Surrey won in two days:

Lockwood bowled creditably, but chief honours were carried by Richardson, who opened the splendid record he obtained against the Australians during the summer by taking eleven wickets for 95 runs.[55]

There were a further eleven, including a hat-trick – his first of four for the county – against Gloucestershire as Surrey again triumphed with a day to spare, five in the first innings against Cambridge University (Lockwood had eight in the second), nine against Lancashire to take him through 50 for the season in less than three weeks.

En route, he had distinguished himself with his batting in the Gloucestershire match.

Richardson, however, proved as useful to Surrey with the bat as he had with the ball. Brockwell and he hit so freely that seventy minutes realised 105 runs, of which Richardson's share was 69. He had one piece of luck in hitting a ball just over point's head which Mr E.M.Grace could have caught had he not left it to Captain Luard who failed to reach it. Otherwise, he gave no chance and his all round hitting was particularly clean and well timed.[56]

The partnership, beginning at 75-9, realised as many as the whole of the Gloucestershire first innings through which W.G.Grace had carried his bat for 61. Richardson never bettered his 69 and never, as a batsman, was he in more distinguished company, as Surrey's No.11 matched Gloucestershire's No.1 as the top scorer for his county. The partnership remains the highest for Surrey's tenth wicket against Gloucestershire and has lasted longer than that for any other wicket. It is Richardson's only appearance in the Surrey record books for his batting, compared with several dozen for his bowling.

The innings seems to have warmed him up for a spell of 18.4-6-33-6 in the second innings:

Richardson's bowling was again accountable for the failure of the Gloucestershire batsmen. This time he was even more successful and on Friday morning his analysis showed 39 balls for seven runs and

---

54   p 81
55   p 183
56   *Cricket* 8 June 1893

four wickets.

His season's best at Bramall Lane followed in a low-scoring match when four completed innings totalled only 320 runs. His nine for 47 in the first innings in 19.4 overs which at one stage included seven for 12 in eight overs, when coupled with Lockwood's eight for 39 in the second innings, would normally have been a match-winning performance, but the Surrey pair were eclipsed by Hirst and Wardall as Yorkshire's 98 and 91 were sufficient to beat the visitors' 72 and 59.

There was still a shadow of suspicion over his action; but the knowledgeable Yorkshire crowd thought it was all right. David Frith has the following anecdote.

> After he had taken 9 for 47 against Yorkshire at Bramall Lane, with the grinders on the terraces barracking him mercilessly, one of them was asked if they resented his success because of any wrongness in his action. "We wish the booger did throw" came the response, "cos then he wouldn't be the booger that he is!"[57]

Several more impressive bowling performances characterised the season and his four for 63 and three for 66 against Nottinghamshire at The Oval, though less spectacular than many, ensured a Bank Holiday double over Surrey's midland rivals. Later in August in a non-first-class match at Grace Road on a pitch which an overnight thunderstorm had rendered 'all in favour of the bowlers'[58] he bowled throughout the match for 11-6-18-6 and 11-5-17-5 in which Surrey's 34 and 64 played Leicestershire's 53 and 56 for 5. Nine wickets against Somerset at The Oval and eleven against Gloucestershire at Clifton College, while not preventing Surrey's first defeat in eight years by the county of the Graces, brought him to the climax of the season.

He had already been selected for the South of England, then for the Players against the Australians and, finally, after little over a season in first-class cricket, for England in the third Test of the summer at Old Trafford. It was a début by default for two of them, neither Richardson nor his Surrey colleague Brockwell having been part of the original selection. But Lockwood had strained his leg and F.S.Jackson preferred to play for Yorkshire who also refused to release Bobby Peel. Richardson did not let his country down, continuing his Surrey form on the international stage, bowling first change behind Mold and Briggs and taking five wickets in each innings. In the first, he took out the upper middle-order of George Giffen, Harry Trott and William Bruce and in the second, had Giffen and Bruce again in addition to opener, Alex Bannerman. The match was drawn, but he had established his international credentials on his way to 174 wickets in the season at 15.4 each (still some way behind J.T.Hearne who had 212), five in an innings on twenty occasions, ten in a match on seven. He had ended the season at the Hastings Festival with six for 43 and seven for 86 for the South against the Australians, then four for 74 and five for 103 for the South against the North. 1893 was simply the prelude to four

---

57   *The First Great Test Series* p 29
58   *Cricket* 17 August 1893

more outstanding home seasons when the statistics became even more impressive and, by modern-day standards, verged on the incredible. From then on his selection for England was as automatic as that for Surrey.

1894

Surrey, still without Lohmann, but with Richardson and Lockwood very much to the fore, were determined to regain what players and members saw as their rightful place at the head of the County Championship and did so in some style. Without the distraction of an Australian tour, they won thirteen and tied one of their sixteen matches. Seventeen wickets in two early season first-class but non-Championship matches against Warwickshire and Derbyshire were a suitable warm-up for a nineteenth-century Whitsuntide equivalent of the Real Madrid-Barcelona *el clásico*. At Trent Bridge, albeit without Gunn and Shrewsbury, Nottinghamshire once again succumbed to Richardson (36.2-22-32-6 and 30.2-3-67-7 – eleven bowled, one lbw) and had lost by an innings by the end of the second day:

> Richardson's bowling was quite the feature of the match. Altogether he took thirteen wickets at a cost of just over seven and a half runs apiece.[59]

Surrey in 1894 – containing four Thames Ditton players –
Maurice Read, Tom Richardson, George Ayres (first three on back row) and
Billy Brockwell (second right on middle row). Richardson's association with the
Club began in 1896, through his friendship with George Ayres and his move to
Thames Ditton on his marriage.
[Thames Ditton Cricket Club 1883 - 2008]

59   *Cricket* 17 May 1894

Gloucestershire were dispatched by an innings and 200 runs, Middlesex by five wickets. An 'eight-for' against Cambridge University at The Oval was followed by yet another against the same opponents at Fenner's a week later.

> On the renewal [ie after lunch] helped to some extent by the wicket, Richardson bowled with remarkable success...

W.G.Druce occupied the crease for an hour and a half for 20, but otherwise

> Richardson bowled with remarkable success..no one faced Richardson with any confidence and his analysis was quite out of the common, showing eight wickets for forty runs...[60]

In full it was 22.1-10-40-8, hardly 'out of the common' by this time – indeed, almost the norm, as illustrated by his 20-5-28-4, 20-4-42-6, 21.4-7-46-5 and 27.3-5-68-7 in substantial wins against Yorkshire and Lancashire.

He celebrated the summer solstice by emulating his nine for 47 of the previous season with ten for 45 against Essex at the The Oval. Only on four other occasions has a bowler taken all ten in a first-class match for Surrey. There have been only 80 instances in the history of first-class cricket.

> The wicket though slow was not difficult and this made Richardson's bowling the more remarkable...Richardson took all ten wickets a feat which has never before been performed by a Surrey bowler. Seven of the batsmen were clean bowled, one (Russell) played on and the other two were caught.[61]

Surrey led by 242 on the first innings at Derby, Richardson and Smith taking five each, but rain prevented their cashing in on that advantage. A defeat by Kent and a win against Somerset followed before Notts and Gloucestershire were once again both beaten by an innings, thanks almost entirely to Richardson's 19-8-39-4, 37.4-11-80-6, 17.5-5-27-6 and 20.1-4-34-7 – and in between another 'seven-for' in a win at Taunton. The spectacular was becoming the norm.

> After Painter had been dismissed, however, at 63, Richardson resumed with such success that in forty-six balls he had five wickets at a cost of only ten runs. How much of the credit rested with Richardson his figures will show. In the match he took thirteen wickets at a cost of little over five and a half runs apiece. To Brockwell and him indeed, Surrey's victory was mainly due.[62]

Brockwell had made 72. Their efforts had not gone unnoticed:

> Mr A.E.Stoddart is apparently impressed with the necessity of having a strong back-bone of Surrey for the team he is to take to Australia next month. Richardson and Lockwood have already signed for the trip, and Brockwell last week accepted the offer made by Mr Stoddart.[63]

---

60   *Cricket* 14 June 1894
61   *Cricket* 21 June 1894
62   *Cricket* 16 August 1894
63   *Cricket* 23 August 1894

Hayward's 142 paved the way for yet another innings victory, this time over Kent, and Richardson's seven for 47, followed by Lockwood's six for 39, finished off the job – revenge for the earlier defeat at Catford Bridge, one of only four in first-class cricket that season.

The bowling of Richardson and Lockwood and Kingsmill Key's captaincy in his first season were undoubtedly major contributors to Surrey's regaining the title. Richardson was one of five players to be awarded his county cap. It could not have caused much debate:

> Richardson proved to be the best bowler of the year, and he was so splendidly backed up by Lockwood that Mr Key's duties were considerably lightened, and at the end of the season he had the proud satisfaction of knowing that his county was at the head of the Championship table ...

> He nursed his bowlers with admirable judgment, and very many good judges are of the opinion that Richardson would never have made his vast reputation if he had been under a man who did not know the precise moment when it was necessary to give him a rest.[64]

Alas, it was not always so in later years.

Wisden summarised the season as follows:

> On all wickets – fast as well as slow – no other county had two bowlers quite so deadly as Richardson and Lockwood, to whom the young left-hander, Smith, proved a most able assistant. Nearly all the bowling work of the season devolved upon these three men, who took amongst them 270 wickets in the championship matches and in all first-class engagements no fewer than 414. No other bowler on the side took more than fourteen in the whole of the season. Of the three bowlers who did so much, Richardson clearly carried off the chief honours. On some days there was nothing to choose between him and Lockwood, but he was more consistently effective than his colleague, and not only took a greater number of wickets, but came out with a far better average. An unfortunate strain, sustained in the Middlesex match at Lord's, kept him out of the eleven for three weeks, or there is no doubt he would have taken considerably over 200 wickets for Surrey during the season. Even at that, his number reached 196. Against Essex at the Oval he took all ten wickets in one innings, a performance which, but for the promotion of Essex, would not have been reckoned in first-class matches. Curiously enough, Richardson did not play in any first-class engagements last season, except those of Surrey, but his doings for the county were sufficient to stamp him as, beyond question, the bowler of the year.[65]

It was the last occasion for four seasons that he would not progress beyond the 200-wicket mark. Having regained the Championship, Surrey formalised the concept of winter pay, though there had been occasional instances for the previous decade and more. They were followed within a

64   *Cricket* 12 April 1900 – *A Chat about Mr K J Key*
65   1895 p 3

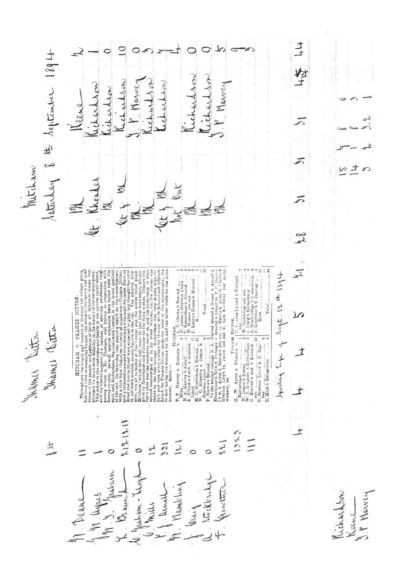

Scorebook and press report – Mitcham v Thames Ditton 1894: Tom 7 – 8.
[Surrey History Centre and Thames Ditton Cricket Club]

couple of years by Lancashire and Yorkshire who had similar aspirations.[66] For Richardson it was £100, but in any case, he had done more than enough to book his passage to Australia.

A busy season in which Richardson had sent down something approaching a thousand overs and taken close on two hundred wickets at little over ten each, taken five in an innings on average every week and ten in a match every fortnight, ended in anticlimax as, in a career that was virtually injury-free, he failed to complete the last, non-first-class match of the season, the star-studded W.W.Read - W.G.Grace bonanza at Reigate Priory.

Brockwell and Richardson opened the bowling:

> Though the latter was unfortunately lame and unable to get up his full pace, he soon got rid of Mr Hewett who had not scored. Richardson's leg, it was found during the interval would not allow him to take the field again (11-5-14-1) ...[67]

It was a limp end to a spectacular year and no guide to what lay ahead in Australia during the winter and the following three seasons.

66   Sissons *The Players* pp 95-99
67   *Cricket* 20 September 1894

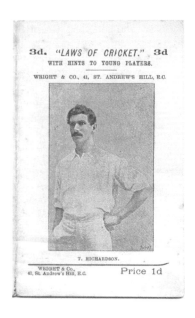

3d. *"LAWS OF CRICKET."* **3d**

WITH HINTS TO YOUNG PLAYERS.

WRIGHT & CO., 41, ST. ANDREW'S HILL, E.C.

T. RICHARDSON.

WRIGHT & Co.,
41, St. Andrew's Hill, E.C.

Price 1d

1894

THOMAS RICHARDSON.

The crack fast bowler was born at Byfleet in Surrey, on August 11, 1870, and first practised the game on Mitcham Green. Several excellent performances in the spring of 1892 brought him under the notice of the county authorities, and he was given a place in the Surrey eleven for their opening match of the season, against Essex, at Kennington Oval. His *debut* was a most successful one, and in the match he secured twelve wickets at an aggregate cost of 100 runs. There was no need for his services to be utilised to any great extent in the summer of 1892, but, during last season, as even our old friend Macaulay's "merest schoolboy" knows, such success as Surrey could boast of were mainly due to his truly remarkable bowling. At the time he met with the accident to his hand at the end of last June, he was at the summit of the bowling averages. Cricket lovers will recall his brilliant achievements last season against Notts, when he secured fourteen wickets at an aggregate cost of 145 runs. Also against Derbyshire he took twelve wickets for 96; the Australian team, eleven for 95; Gloucestershire, eleven for 77; and Yorkshire, ten for 82, with more than common pleasure. In Surrey's opening match of last season against Warwickshire at the Oval, he dismissed four batsmen with consecutive balls, and got seven wickets for 44 runs in the visitors' second innings. He has also proved himself to be a tower of strength to his county at a time when in the absence of Lohmann, Surrey's prospects are none too bright. His performance on Whitsun Monday, too, at Nottingham, against Notts, was quite the feature of the match, taking altogether thirteen wickets at a cost of just over seven and half runs a piece. Richardson is tall, deeply bronzed, sombre - moustached as a son of the sunny South, reticent, believes that " on their own merits, modest men are dumb," and, when questioned as to his experiences, thinks that his cricket career has been so short that he could say but little that would be of interest to the public. He is a right-handed bowler with a high delivery, that gets up quickly off the pitch. It would seem that as a manipulator of the leather he has come to stay, while at times he shows himself to be useful with the willow.

Card on Richardson's achievements to 1894 sold for 1d.
[Surrey Cricket Library and Archive]

Chapter Four
Australia 1894/95

One for 85 and one for 41 against South Australia at Adelaide and one for 92 and none for 45 against Victoria at Melbourne, following on, was no portent of what was to come. Tom had bowled a few overs en route in the traditional non-first-class match against Ceylon and played but did not bowl in a similarly unclassified match against Gawlor. The Adelaide match had been an inauspicious start for the tourists as they went down by six wickets, but the Victoria match was won by 134 runs, Briggs and Peel sharing sixteen wickets between them.

Then, in a decision that looks surprisingly anachronistic at a time when key bowlers were expected to perform almost non-stop,

> Mr Stoddart decided to rest Richardson who will have to be nursed for the big matches.[68]

Tom missed the New South Wales match and that against Twenty-two of Toowoomba, though he was given an outing against Twenty-two of New England at Armidale when he had nine for 46. But the rest seems to have worked and he came back with an impressive performance against Queensland, first-class but not yet participating in the recently established Sheffield Shield, as, spearheaded by Tom's bowling, Stoddart's team demolished their hosts by an innings and 274 runs. Tom had returned to something like his expected form with 18.1-5-52-8 and 8-2-11-3, ten of his victims being bowled, the other lbw.

> Richardson and Peel bowled unchanged although it did seem that Bobby was kept on too long. The "Surrey catapult" secured the fine average of 8 for 52 which will go a long way to pulling up his general averages which were knocked all to pieces at Adelaide and Melbourne… wonderful figures on a perfect pitch.[69]

And so to what David Frith has called 'The First Great Test Series' – a five-match rubber for the first time for a decade, though there had been seven Anglo-Australian 'series' of one, two or three matches. The venues were identical, two matches at Melbourne, two at Sydney and one at Adelaide, though not in the same order, as, coincidentally was the results pattern – two wins by England, two by Australia and a final win for England to take the series 3-2.

There were other matches in between, minor ones against Bendigo, Ballarat and Stawell and a first-class fixture against a combined New South Wales-Queensland XI at Brisbane. Richardson played a full part in the latter but

---

68   *Cricket* 31 January 1895
69   *Cricket* 31 January 1895

A.E.Stoddart's team to Australia 1894/95.
[Roger Mann Collection]

was used sparingly in the others, a sensible policy given the amount of bowling he was required to do in the Tests – almost 300 overs in the five matches.

The pattern was set in the First Test at Sydney when he bowled 55.3 overs, taking five for 181 in an Australian total which, thanks to a century by Giffen, a double century by Gregory and a partnership of over 150 for the ninth wicket between the latter and Blackham, reached 586. Richardson was clearly overbowled: his pace was effective early in the innings, indeed well into the second day, but towards the end he wilted in the Antipodean heat.

> Runs came slowly off Richardson, who was bowling better than he had before he took the wickets at Brisbane....Richardson bowled well, while Peel and Briggs were fearfully expensive without gaining a wicket...

> Richardson and Peel resumed the bowling, and a ball from the former rose as high as Reedman's head. The batsman foolishly cut at it, and Brockwell in the slips had a chance which he did not accept...

> Again one of Richardson's rose and clouted Reedman on the head...

> a fast ball from Richardson landed at the base of McLeod's middle stump...

> Runs came apace, yet Richardson and Peel still bowled on as they had while 132 runs were put on. It was simply killing Richardson, whose pace had dropped considerably, and both batsmen were able to hit him to leg to their heart's content.[70]

Lockwood, meanwhile, had bowled three overs.

However, from being on their knees and obliged to follow on, England staged a remarkable recovery to win by ten runs, the only instance of victory after following on until Botham's match at Headingley in 1981. Australia's 586 remains the highest total by a losing side in Test cricket. Giffen, after his double century, then emulated Richardson by bowling 43 overs in the first innings, 75 in the second and still finished on the losing side in this 'timeless' Test, the first to go into a sixth day. Bobby Peel was the eventual match winner with six for 67. Richardson's earlier efforts had taken their toll:

> Richardson was suffering from a severe cold and only went out in order that he might have a good sweat.[71]

At a time when off-the-field activities attract less press publicity than they do nowadays, those of Lockwood in Sydney harbour were something of an exception, paralleling perhaps the Flintoff pedalo incident more than a century later:

> An untoward accident happened to Lockwood and it was only by the merest fluke that his life was saved. The incident was kept very quiet

---

70   *Cricket* 31 January 1895
71   *Cricket* 31 January 1895

but leaked out some days afterwards. The Englishmen were being taken round the beautiful Sydney Harbour. They drew up after lunch in one of the lovely little bays which abound. Straightaway Lockwood jumped overboard despite previous warnings as to the prevalence of sharks, and essayed to swim ashore, a distance of at least 100 yards. When midway across he called out for assistance three or four times, and, thinking it was a joke, those on board took little notice. A yacht was, however, passing, and seeing that the Englishman was struggling, threw two life buoys towards him. He secured one but went under, his feet going up in the air. Then a couple of yachtsmen came to his assistance, and got him ashore. With the aid of brandy the Surrey cricketer soon came round, though the serious nature of the affair left an uncomfortable impression on all.[72]

The New Year Test at Melbourne provided the first instance of a Test captain inviting the opposition to bat and the second instance in as many matches of England recovering from a seemingly impossible position to win. A heavy thunderstorm on the day before the match made batting conditions difficult and the captains agreed that the pitch should be rolled after each day's play. MacLaren was out to the first ball of the match and England were all out for 75 in 40.1 overs and two hours in their first innings thus entirely vindicating Giffen's decision.

'Richardson's fast ones bumped a great deal', but by the second day 'the wicket looked excellent except for a spot at one end'. Led by Stoddart's second innings 175, England were able to set Australia a fourth innings target of over four hundred which, thanks in part to Richardson's 60-10-100-2 on top of his first innings 23-6-57-5, the hosts never looked like achieving.

This was one of the rare occasions on which Richardson's batting was complimented. He was able to cash in on what was perhaps tired bowling. 53 had been added for the ninth wicket. Then –

> Richardson, the last man, also gave a lot of trouble and the score was raised to 475 before a fine catch in the deep by Gregory dismissed Richardson.[73]

His 11 was still the lowest score in an innings in which all the batsmen reached double figures. *Cricket* was to say of him later that he was

> anything but a scientific batsman, though he could hit like a horse kicking.[74]

On to Adelaide for the Third Test, with Australia needing to win to stay in a series which had sparked nationwide enthusiasm. Daily attendance at the MCG had been around 15,000 and the interest spilled over:

> Intense interest was taken in the match throughout Australia, and in South Australia itself where the match was played, special trains were

---

72   *Cricket* 31 January 1895
73   *Cricket* 28 February 1895
74   Obituary 20 July 1912

run into the city, while fully 500 people journeyed nearly 500 miles by rail from Melbourne to Adelaide especially to see the match...

Friday was a terrible day with the thermometer at 155 deg in the sun and 102 deg in the shade...

Then at 124 a splendid longer ball from Richardson clean beat Harry. Richardson had now taken four wickets for 57...

His pace was terrific and the pitch wonderfully accurate...

Richardson bowled with tremendous energy...[75]

Nevertheless, his performances of 21-4-75-5 and 31.2-8-89-3 were insufficient to prevent an Australian victory by the large margin of 382 runs.

In the Fourth Test, back at Sydney, Australia levelled the series, stuffing England out of sight in under two days playing time, bowling them out twice on the third scheduled day, after the second had been lost to rain. Richardson had bowled well, but without much luck, he and England suffering from missed chances:

At 81 Richardson went on against the wind, and Briggs changed ends. Now came the turning point in the game. With the total at 84, of which Graham had made 37, the dashing batsman snicked a ball from Richardson straight at Brockwell, just a nice height to catch, but the fieldsman let it drop... With his score at 29, Darling lifted one from Richardson right into the hands of MacLaren at long-on, but though that fieldsman had not to move for the ball, he failed to hold it.[76]

Despite Richardson's participation in the highest partnership of either of England's miserable innings – 20 for the ninth wicket, Lockwood being absent hurt – the only effect was to reduce the margin of defeat to an innings and 147 runs.

The final match of the rubber with the series tied at 2-2, was a much closer affair and a triumph for Richardson and, eventually, England. Richardson had now become the benchmark against which other batsmen and bowlers were measured

Iredale... played Richardson much better than anyone on the side...

Richardson was able to make the ball "kick" a good deal which several of the batsmen in this match were painfully aware of, few of them escaping one or more blows from him.

Richardson fairly triumphed over the batsmen and executed a feat worthy of the reputation he has achieved in the Old Country.[77]

42-7-138-3 and 45.2-7-104-6 supported by Peel's 48-13-114-4 and 46-16-89-3 left England with a none-too-straightforward target of just under

---

75   *Cricket* 28 February 1895
76   *Cricket* 28 March 1895
77   *Cricket* 11 April 1895

three hundred which, thanks to a third-wicket partnership of 210 between Albert Ward and John Brown, they reached with six wickets to spare.

Away from the cricket, the press was beginning to take an interest in off-the-field activities.

> A MELBOURNE paper, I notice, has been correcting a statement that Richardson, the Surrey bowler was engaged to an Armidale heiress. The correction was perhaps quite well made for Richardson who has a nice little wife, is the picture of health, and the author of any such canard would have a bad time of it if he came within striking distance of "our Tom". Equal reliance is no doubt to be placed on the announcement that Brockwell, who was the victim of one quite uncalled-for insinuation with regard to Iredale and Surrey cricket, paid marked attention to a fair Jewess, whose sister is the wife of a famous Surrey cricketer.[78]

Richardson was not in fact married until October of that year, but more seriously, Rev R.S.Holmes summed up the cricketing side of the trip:

> This tour has completed the good work done by Lord Sheffield's team three years ago. Public interest in cricket was at it lowest point in Australia; now it has touched high-water mark.

> Richardson has done as well as any bowler which is, perhaps, a very flattering compliment, seeing that no bowling analysis will come out at under 20 runs a wicket. His chief successes were in the Brisbane match, and in the last match against Australia. He was at his very best and there is no better. He was a terror to Giffen this tour.[79]

Conventional wisdom is that fast bowlers hunt in pairs as Turner and Ferris had in earlier years demonstrated for Australia and Richardson and Lockwood did for Surrey. But Lockwood was little used in this series and such support as Richardson had came from Peel and to a lesser extent Briggs, leaving him to plough a lone furrow as the main strike bowler. Richardson had 32 wickets at 26.53 in 291.2 overs; Peel 27 at 26.7 in 305.1; Briggs 15 at 29.06 in 150.3; Lockwood 5 at 67.8 in 123.5.

In financial terms too, the tour was successful. In contrast to the previous one in 1891/92 which left Lord Sheffield out of pocket by about £3,000,[80] Stoddart's tour made a profit of £7,000. Income from the fifth, deciding, Test alone was £4,000...

> All of which goes to show that, properly conducted, and with a certain amount of luck, cricket tours in Australia are not a bad investment. In this case, too, it is evidently satisfactory that the profits go to the Melbourne CC and the New South Wales Cricket Association which means that they will go towards the development of the game in Australia generally.[81]

---

78   *Cricket* 16 May 1895
79   *Cricket* 28 March 1895
80   *The Australasian* 2 April 1892
81   *Cricket* 16 May 1895

Wisden recognised England's outstanding performance and the importance of Richardson's contribution - once he had adapted to the very different conditions.

> It is perfectly safe to say that since the visit of George Parr's eleven in 1863-64 no tour of English cricketers in Australia has been from every point of view more brilliantly successful than that of Mr Stoddart's team. In the series of contests with All Australia they had won the rubber by three matches to two. Never, probably, have five matches excited more widespread interest. They drew such crowds of people to the Australian grounds that the Melbourne Club and the trustees of the Sydney ground, under whose joint auspices the tour was undertaken, divided between them a profit of about seven thousand pounds. In England the interest was greater than had ever been felt in matches played away from our own shores, the enterprise of the *Pall Mall Gazette*, in arranging every afternoon when the big matches were in progress for long cable messages, keeping lovers of the game in this country in closer touch with cricket in Australia than they had ever been before.
>
> It was Richardson's wonderful bowling that first made victory probable in the last test match. So difficult did the Surrey fast bowler find it to accommodate himself to the beautifully true fast grounds that the first three wickets he took in the Colonies cost him about a hundred runs each.[82]

---

82   *Wisden* 1896 p 367

Chapter Five
1895...Annus Mirabilis...Surrey

Surrey looked forward to the new season – and beyond - with an optimism that proved entirely justified.

> Surrey seems to possess at the present time a stronger and more capable array of players than any other county. Lockwood, Richardson, Hayward, Baldwin, Brockwell, Ayres, Street, Marshall; all these are men who ought to do splendid service for years. Nor must it be forgotten that some of the most capable University men owe allegiance to Surrey – Mr C.M.Wells, Mr C.B.Fry and Mr G.O.Smith, the Carthusian, prominent among them... and, if not next year, in a year or two's time after that Surrey will (we prophesy) again hold the championship. [83]

The prophesy was not far wrong. Outstanding performance followed outstanding performance as, spearheaded by Richardson's bowling, buoyed by Lohmann's return, and supported by Abel, Holland and Maurice and Walter Read with the bat, Surrey retained the title they had surrendered on only one occasion since 1890. By the end of the season, Tom had taken five wickets or more in an innings on 36 occasions, ten or more in a match on 17, averaging about nine per match, and had established himself as the leading fast bowler of his generation, maybe of all time.

At the end of May, for the first time since 1866, Surrey took on the full might of England at The Oval in a match arranged for Walter Read's testimonial.

The bowling honours were taken by Arthur Pougher with nine for 34 as Surrey collapsed to 85 all out in their way to a defeat by an innings and 75 runs. In true benefit-match tradition Surrey used nine bowlers, but inevitably Richardson was the main one, finishing with 43.1-9-103-6 and polishing off the England tail:

> Richardson soon finished off the innings his analysis after lunch being two overs and a ball for three runs and three wickets.[84]

Cricket reporting at the time was factual rather than analytical and tended to devote more space to feats of batsmanship rather than outstanding bowling performances, but when a bowler takes 290 wickets in a season, it is unlikely that he will not receive an occasional mention. Thus, Warwickshire at Edgbaston –

> in their first attempt did but poorly against Richardson who had seven wickets, five bowled, for just over seven runs apiece. Only two

83   *Cricket* 16 May 1895
84   *Cricket* 30 May 1895

Warwickshire men played with confidence although the pitch was in excellent condition.[85]

Then against Gloucestershire at The Oval,

Only Lockwood and Richardson failed to score double figures.

In fact, they made three and one respectively in a total of 405, but more than compensated for that perceived failure by taking seventeen wickets between them.

Richardson quickly finished off the innings by catching Bracher and bowling Roberts, so that Surrey won by an innings and 195 runs.[86]

At Bradford,

Then Richardson went on after a rest, and with only 31 runs added four of the best Yorkshire wickets had fallen when they ceased play for the day ... Richardson clean bowled three men and Smith accounted for the rest.[87]

Ranjitsinhji, when asked about the best bowlers of his day, was only slightly equivocal.

I can hardly say. Many are very good but Mold and Richardson among fast bowlers seem to me most dangerous, and of slow bowlers, I should unhesitatingly say that Peel is foremost.[88]

Against Derbyshire at The Oval,

Richardson's last piece of bowling was 7 overs, 4 maidens, 15 runs, 4 wickets[89]

The conventional wisdom that Richardson was unable to bowl on wet pitches was exploded at Catford:

One of the most dismal batting failures was that of the Kent eleven at Catford on Monday.

When rain brought the first day to a premature close, Surrey were 59 for none in reply to Kent's 43 all out, the sixth, seventh, eighth and ninth wickets all falling at 42. Then, a bit of a contribution with the bat: Richardson did not believe in wasting too much time on his batting and his innings were often short and explosive, his philosophy being the time-honoured maxim that tail enders should hit out and/or get out.

Richardson then hit out and made 23 of 28 for the last wicket in a quarter of an hour.[90]

The rout then resumed.

85   *Cricket* 6 June 1895
86   *Cricket* 13 June 1895
87   *Cricket* 20 June 1895
88   *Cricket* 20 June 1895
89   *Cricket* 25 July 1895
90   *Cricket* 25 July 1895

Richardson and Lohmann as on the previous day could not be resisted, and no one of the last nine batsmen reached double figures ... Lohmann's re-appearance was quite successful, he obtaining in all nine wickets for 90, but Richardson had ten for 66.[91]

It presaged the Lord's Test of the following season when Lohmann and Richardson were again an effective combination. Some years later, Douglas Jardine was to write:

People say they used 'to go and see Lohmann and Richardson bowl'. Today does anyone go to see anyone bowl?[92]

Only for a couple of seasons when Lohmann's appearances were spasmodic did he and Richardson bowl in tandem, but when they did the results were, almost without exception, devastating.

Richardson's pace continued unabated:

The cricket critics have very properly pointed out that Richardson's performance at The Oval last Thursday in the Sussex match, in bowling Mr Murdoch, with a ball that sent the bail fifty yards is not even the best of the season.[93]

That distinction apparently fell to Charles Kortright bowling for Essex against Leicestershire at Leyton, but the longest recorded was 62 yards by H.Rotherham when he bowled Mr D.H.Docker in the Uppingham Rovers v Gentlemen of Derbyshire match at Derby in August 1881. Anorakism had been born.[94]

More significant perhaps than the distance travelled by the bail was Tom's best bowling return of the season – nine for 49 - and a breezy 41 not out. Then, against Derbyshire, he again combined with Lohmann in another innings victory.

Lohmann and Richardson bowled on a wicket which helped them with startling effect. In the whole match Lohmann had eight wickets for 59 and Richardson eleven for 60, these men bowling unchanged.[95]

A week later, Rev R.S.Holmes commented:

Surrey's single innings victory over Derbyshire, although they lost the toss again, had just two prominent characteristics – an innings of 50 by Hayward, and two bowlers unchanged. Lohmann and Richardson had never combined before in this way, although both of them had a hand on the four previous occasions on which this same unusual distinction had fallen to the bowlers since 1873, Lohmann figuring three times, Richardson once.[96]

The consistency of wicket-taking continued, his back-to-back returns

91   *Cricket* 25 July 1895
92   Letter to *The Times* 5 July 1947
93   *Cricket* 1 August 1895
94   *Cricket* 1 August 1895: the text reads 'Effingham', but the strong likelihood is that it should be 'Uppingham'
95   *Cricket* 1 August 1895
96   *Cricket* 8 August 1895

in innings victories against Sussex and Hampshire inside a week were representative of his effort and penetration – 35-10-71-6, 40-12-108-6, then 34.2-9-85-6, 29.2-7-70-9. The two victories ensured that Surrey were once again winners of the County Championship.

> Richardson bowled nearly as well as ever, taking 12 wickets at just under 15 runs a-piece. Surrey and Yorkshire cricketers may be stale from overwork, if there is such a complaint in cricket; it is surprising, however, that the man who has worked harder than any two others, seems as fresh as new paint, and might only just be starting the season instead of winding it up with more wickets than any other English bowler has bagged in any previous season.[97]

Twenty-two wickets in two matches at the Hastings Festival brought his season's total to 290. For Stoddart's Anglo-Australian XI against the Rest of England

> Peel and Richardson soon put England out of their misery, and all the side went down for 44, a remarkable finish to a remarkable season...[98]

'Richardson has accomplished a marvellous performance with the ball,' enthused *Cricket*.[99] – and in a batsman's year when W.G.Grace scored a thousand runs in May, the first to do so.

Once again, the season came to a light-hearted conclusion at the Reigate Festival:

> Both teams included many well-known players, but there was no attempt to send them in the usual order adopted in county matches, lots being drawn for priority. Thus, when W.G.Grace won the toss, and decided that his side should bat first, Richardson, the Surrey fast bowler who had good fortune in the draw, had the honour of going in first with W L Murdoch.[100]

He made 16 before being bowled by Bobby Peel. He did not bowl. Maybe he had bowled enough that season as his first-class figures of 1691.1-463-4170-290 might indicate.[101] The 290 wickets in an English season, beating Turner's 283 in 1888 was to stand as a record until passed by 'Tich' Freeman in 1928. In 31 first-class games, Richardson had taken ten or more wickets in a match in no fewer than 17, including all of the last eight and twelve of the last fourteen.

Too much should not be read into trans-generation comparisons, particularly when they relate to different types of bowlers, but it may be worth a mention that Richardson obtained his wickets at a lower average and strike rate, 14.37 against 18.05 and 29.15 against 39. Freeman's economy rate was 2.77, against Richardson's 2.95.[102] His overall career

---

97   *Cricket* 5 September 1895
98   *Cricket* 19 September 1895
99   5 September 1895
100   *Cricket* 19 September 1895
101   1,691.1 overs confirmed by CricketArchive and by *Wisden* until 1954. Since then *Wisden* has had 1,690.1.
102   2.46 converted to six-ball over equivalent

*The ball presented by Surrey CCC to Tom Richardson
on the occasion of his marriage in October 1895.*

*The Inscription reads: "This ball in the Bridegroom's hands obtained 4
wickets in one over. May the happiness of Mr & Mrs Richardson's
married life abound in the same degree."
[Surrey CCC Library and Archive]*

economy rate was 2.94, so to that extent it was a fairly typical season. That would not have concerned Richardson in the least. He bowled to take wickets and his idea of containment was to get a batsman back in the pavilion where he could score no more. Furthermore, there is no record of how many of the runs he conceded were scored accidentally from the edge of the bat, though his colleague George Lohmann suggested it might be about a third of them.[103]

Rev R.S.Holmes had little time for maiden overs and compared the contributions of Peel and Richardson to the season:

> I never could see anything wonderful about a succession of maiden overs, except it is wonderful that a man supposed to have brains, can convert himself into a bowling machine. Look at the bowling for the present season. Richardson has had just two and a half runs scored off every over he has bowled; Peel who has sent down about the same number of overs, has been hit about to the tune of one and a half runs per over. But Richardson has taken 100 more wickets than Peel. For this reason I would prefer him to any living bowler, although it is perhaps not fair to compare, or rather contrast, two bowlers whose methods are so completely unlike.[104]

Once again *Wisden* had no doubts about the significance of Tom's contribution to Surrey's retention of the Championship:

> While nearly all the players met with more or less success, the fine record gained by the county was chiefly due to Richardson's wonderful

103   Bettesworth *Chats on the Cricket Field; George Lohmann* 30 July 1896
104   *Cricket* 12 September 1895

bowling and the exceptionally fine batting of Abel. To praise either of the two men beyond his deserts would be almost impossible. Of the two, however, Richardson was the more indispensable to the eleven. Even had Abel – instead of surpassing all he had ever done for Surrey-enjoyed only an ordinary season, the batting of the team would have been strong, but any failure on Richardson's part might at once have involved disaster. Up to the time of Lohmann's return to the eleven towards the end of July, Richardson had all the weight of the bowling on his shoulders, Lockwood's loss of form leaving him with far less support than he might reasonably have expected. However, he was more than equal to the occasion, bowling day after day on true, fast, run-getting wickets in a way that can seldom have been approached. It was feared that the hard work he had gone through with Mr Stoddart's team in Australia might affect his pace and spin, but so far from this being the case he proved himself, if possible, an even finer bowler than in 1894. With Lohmann's return, Richardson was naturally much better off, and it so happened that at the same time the weather broke up and the wickets began to give the bowlers the advantage. It was the crowning proof of Richardson's exceptional excellence, however, that many of his finest performances were accomplished on wickets that afforded him no assistance. Only on one or two occasions did he show any signs of losing his form, and despite the great amount of bowling he had to do, he left off in September apparently as fresh and strong as at the beginning of the season.[105]

He was now an invaluable member of the Surrey and England side, a match-winner on numerous occasions. Consequently, he was in a strong negotiating position and along with Lohmann, who had been the first Surrey player to do so in 1891, and Hayward, was able to secure a 'star' contract stretching beyond the usual single year and embracing regular winter pay, a concept first introduced in 1894, though there had been spasmodic instances for a decade or so before that. The contract was embodied in an agreement embracing

> the usual summer wages, match fees, talent money and bonus plus a lump sum for one hundred pounds to cover and include all winter pay.[106]

The £100 would be reduced to £50 should winter employment elsewhere for a period exceeding two months be accepted. It was the intention that the arrangement be renewed for as long as Richardson continued to play for the Surrey Club and while the Committee could not commit its successors, a benefit match before 1900 would also be a probability...

Richardson was happy to accept.

---

105   1896 p 3
106   Surrey C C C minutes 1 August 1895

Commonside, Mitcham
Sept 4 1895

I feel I can safely leave my interests in your hands ... I shall therefore for the future consider Surrey to have the first call on my services no matter how flattering any offer is that may be held out to me.[107]

At the end of that season, Richardson married and moved to Thames Ditton, living in Angel Road. The exact location has not been identified, as houses which carried names at the time have subsequently been numbered; but wherever it was, if it was not exactly spitting distance from, it was certainly adjacent to and within easy walking distance of Giggs Hill Green, the home of Thames Ditton Cricket Club and *The Angel* public house at the end of the road which served as the Club's headquarters and venue for its dinners and concerts. Like Mitcham, its major rival, it was a nursery for the county club and among a number of distinguished players who represented Thames Ditton are Tom Hayward, Bill Brockwell, Len Braund, Bill Lockwood, Maurice Read and John Sharpe.

Marriage certificate.

Tom Richardson's name could now be added to that list. George Ayres, who had made his first-class début for Surrey in the same year as Tom and had been a witness at his wedding and probably best man, was doubtless instrumental in persuading the fast bowler, now at the height of his career, to switch his allegiance from Mitcham to their rivals whose ground was conveniently situated at the end of the road in which he had made his new home. He turned out when his county commitments allowed it, served on the club committee and had plenty to say. He was also on the ground committee and at times helped with the preparation of the club's pitches.[108]

---

107   Surrey C C C minutes   5 September 1895
108   Ashton, *Thames Ditton Cricket Club*

Chapter Six

1896...Annus Mirabilis...England

Lillywhite's repeated what it had said in previous years about Richardson, namely

> One of the very best fast bowlers of the day, keeps a good length, and comes back at times a good lot; can bat well and is a good field.[109]

but, although the Annual has plenty to say about public school and university cricket, his performances for Surrey barely rate a mention:

> Lockwood was quite out of form in the latter matches, and the loss of his bowling was felt severely. Richardson and Lohmann, as it was, had to do most of the bowling, and though the former was not quite as successful as in 1895, considering that the wickets gave little assistance on the whole, both Lohmann and he did very well.[110]

Other than that, he is mentioned only in *en passant* or in general terms:

> In respect of the test matches, their surprising collapse at Lord's at the commencement of the first of the three fixtures seriously prejudiced their chances of winning the rubber...

> On some grounds the long spell of fine weather made the pitches so fiery that batsmen could not touch fast bowling, and then the great pace of such bowlers as Jones the Australian and Richardson told with deadly effect...

> [The Australians'] one victory in the test matches was the result of excellent all round cricket, and they won thoroughly on their merits as the game went. The comparatively poor show of the England bowlers on that occasion with the exception of Richardson...[111]

1896 turned out to be a momentous year, starting with a charity match on April Fools Day in which Richardson played an active fund-raising role. He captained a team of Surrey professionals against one of comic entertainers at Thames Ditton to raise funds for the Thames Ditton and Surbiton Cottage Hospital

> During the afternoon the players took round collecting boxes... Richardson himself reminding the spectators that they never knew when they might be there themselves.[112]

A pre-season warm-up saw the county's first string beaten by eight wickets

---

109   1897 p 259
110   p 56
111   pp 17,53, 54
112   *Daily Mail* 2 April 1896

Surrey 1896.
Standing: R.Abel, W.W.Read, W.Brockwell, A.E.Street, F.Boyington (scorer),
F.E.Smith, G.A.Lohmann, G.W.Ayres, H.Wood. Seated: W.H.Lockwood,
T.Richardson, K.J.Key (captain), T.W.Hayward.
[Surrey County Cricket Club]

by the Next XVII, Richardson returning a modest 22-6-63-3 and 5-1-7-1, not, as *Cricket* correctly predicted, the shape of things to come:

> The downfall of the Surrey team in their match against the Next Seventeen is not likely to awaken any great hopes by other counties, that the eleven is played out. Richardson was not in form then, but it is by no means likely that he is going to be a failure this year; he is not the sort of bowler who collapses. Lohmann will soon be on the scene, and if reports are to be trusted, he is as good as ever. It is true that Surrey could do with two or three new bowlers, but there are several men who may reasonably be hoped to come to the front.[113]

For Surrey and for Richardson, the season started well:

> It is not often that a bowler is fortunate enough to secure a wicket, and a good wicket, with the first ball of the season for his county. It was Richardson's experience this year for Surrey. Selected to commence the bowling on Monday in the opening match at the Oval, he sent down for a start one which knocked Walter Quaife's middle stump out of the perpendicular...[114]

He eventually finished with 37-15-71-3 and 32-14-54-5 as Surrey beat Warwickshire by an innings and 26 runs, then in the following match proceeded to demolish Leicestershire by an innings and 259 runs, bowling unchanged through both innings, 20.1-11-31-7 and 28.3-8-82-8:

> C.E.de Trafford ... after making 72 out of 96, he was caught by the wicket-keeper standing back, and then the end soon came. Richardson

---

113   *Cricket* 7 May 1896
114   *Cricket* 7 May 1896

did the hat-trick by bowling Pougher, Geeson and Coe with consecutive balls.

In his 'horse-kicking' mode he had shared a tenth-wicket partnership of 56 with his captain, Kingsmill Key. It was a measure of Surrey's complete dominance that this was one more than the total of Leicestershire's first innings. The pattern of the previous season continued. Of Richardson's 23 wickets in the first two Championship matches of the year, eighteen were bowled.

It was the prelude to two outstanding performances in the Test matches of that season and concluding with the players' strike that saw the end of George Lohmann's career and a hiatus in Richardson's.

Bowling in tandem, Lohmann and Richardson demolished Australia in the First Test at Lord's – 53 all out in 22.3 overs. The tourists did rather better in the second innings, but not well enough to prevent an England victory and not before Richardson had produced another of his marathon spells, 47-15-134-5, J.T.Hearne taking the other five.

> At the beginning of the innings, Richardson seemed to offer no difficulty to Donnan and Darling; his pitch was not at all accurate. Lohmann, on the other hand, was difficult from the first.

Trott ... was completely beaten by Richardson who by this time got a better pitch.

> [Gregory] played with confidence and he and Darling made several fine hits off Richardson, with whom W.G. had a little talk. This was the turning point of the game and thereafter Lohmann and Richardson carried everything before them. Gregory was beaten by Richardson by an extremely fast ball, which seemed, judging by his look when he found that he was bowled, to be altogether a surprise to him. With the next ball, Graham was bowled – another great surprise. Then, after Darling made a lovely cut for four off Richardson, the Surrey bowler sent him a very fast ball which just took off a bail.

> ... There was no longer any room for doubting that the rot was complete. None of the rest of the team even looked like making a stand, and the innings was over in an hour and a quarter. Everybody was asking everybody else for an explanation of the collapse, but none was forthcoming. The bowlers bowled splendidly, it is true, but the ball did not kick or do anything very dreadful; probably the bowling of Richardson was found to be more difficult than had been seen on Australian wickets.[115]

Between the Test matches, indeed between the Hampshire match at Southampton in which he took ten wickets and the Gentlemen v Players match at The Oval in which he took a further ten, Surrey having no fixture, Richardson went off to play some club cricket with Andover and completely ruined the match as a contest. Quite how he came to be playing for Andover is a matter of speculation; perhaps it was his friendship with

---

115   *Cricket* 25 June 1896

George Lohmann who had Andover connections or maybe someone had had a word with him at Southampton. Nevertheless –

> SEVEN wickets with consecutive balls in any class of cricket is a rarity akin to the black tulip. The credit of the latest incident of this kind belongs to Tom Richardson, Surrey's fast bowler. It was done for Andover against Basingstoke on Saturday week. In Basingstoke's first innings he took ten out of eleven wickets – the match was twelve a side. Seven of these were with consecutive balls, and the last six were clean bowled.[116]

The next Test at Old Trafford saw even more bowling for the seemingly tireless fast bowler. Lohmann did not play. Reports vary as to whether he was absent because of injury, illness or personal reasons, but whatever the cause it meant less support for Richardson who bowled over a hundred overs this time, causing Neville Cardus to flash back to the match when writing of the Lancashire-Surrey match at Old Trafford twenty-six years later.

He set the scene – Australia 412 all out, England following on, Ranjitsinhji's 154 not out taking the match into a fourth innings, leaving the tourists 125 to win. A steady start by Australia, 20 for the first wicket before the attention, in a classic piece of purple prose, turns to England and Surrey strike bowler:

> Then it was that Richardson's face was seen to be grim – his customary happy smile gone. In Australia's first innings he had bowled 68 overs for seven wickets and 168 runs. Yet he was here again, bowling like a man just born to immortal energy. And four Australian wickets were down for 45 in an hour. If only England had given the Australians a few more runs, the crowd wished out of its heart – if only Richardson could keep up his pace for another hour. But, of course, no man could expect him to bowl in this superhuman vein for long. Thus did the crowd sigh and regret. But Richardson's spirit did go on burning a dazzling flame. The afternoon moved slowly to the sunset – every hour an eternity. And Richardson *did* bowl and bowl and bowl, and his fury diminished not a jot. Other English bowlers faltered, but not Richardson. The fifth wicket fell at 79, the sixth at 95, the seventh at 100.

Cardus then continued,

> With nine runs still to be got by Australia, Kelly gave a chance to Lilley at the wicket and Lilley let the ball drop to the earth. The heart of Richardson might have burst at this, but it did not. To the end he strove and suffered.

Australia had won by three wickets, and Cardus goes on to describe how, after the players had returned to the pavilion Richardson simply remained at the bowling crease unable to believe that England had failed to win.

> That afternoon Richardson had laboured three mortal hours without surcease. In the match he had bowled 110 overs and three balls, for

---

13 wickets and 244 runs. He never bowled again in a test match at Manchester.[117]

As often with Cardus, it is the style rather than the substance which commands attention and a certain amount of poetic licence has to be allowed. He was eight years old at the time.

Cricket said much the same, but rather more prosaically.

> Richardson alone seemed likely to get wickets and he rose to the occasion in a truly remarkable manner....

> Richardson kept steadily on, and frequently missed the wicket by a hair's breadth – it was one of those days, which all bowlers know so well, when the ball would do anything except hit the wicket. Every now and then, however, he broke through the defence of a batsman and a wicket fell although he enjoyed little rest (this could not be helped for in him the hope of England lay) and he was as difficult at the end of the innings as he was when he began to bowl.

> .... a very great performance, since he had practically nobody who could help him.[118]

The reality of Richardson's actions at the end of the Test is rather more basic than the Cardus version. Drawing on the eye-witness account of one who was there, David Frith describes how Richardson raced from the field and downed two pints of ale before the rest of the team had removed their boots.[119]

The match finished on a Saturday evening. No Sunday cricket in those days of course, but after that Herculean effort at Old Trafford, it must have been something of a relief to Richardson when Surrey won the toss and batted against Middlesex at Lord's the following Monday. Nevertheless, once Surrey were out for 300 (in the popular cliché, Richardson, not unusually, failed to trouble the scorers), he was in action again by the end of the day on his way to 28-6-82-5 and as Middlesex were 141 short of the Surrey total and obliged to follow on – compulsory then in the event of a deficit of 120 or more, the option of batting again to 'rest' his bowlers was not available to Kingsmill Key. Richardson then bowled through the second innings, 15-5-37-5, leading his county to a victory by an innings and 58 runs. At least it gave him and his colleagues a day off before twelve wickets at Catford Bridge.

A defeat by the Australians and a win against Yorkshire followed. During the latter match, Richardson sailed through 200 first-class wickets for the third consecutive season and then produced another of his destructive performances before a capacity attendance in the traditional Bank Holiday fixture against Nottinghamshire at The Oval.

> Before an enormous crowd, numbering about 28,000, Notts enjoyed the privilege of batting first on Bank Holiday; but partly owing to a

---

117   *A Cricketer's Book* pp 46-49
118   23 July 1896
119   *Caught England, Bowled Australia* p 196

little trickiness in the wicket, partly due to some splendid bowling by Richardson and partly due to lifeless batting, they could make very little headway. In fact, their first innings was something like that of the first innings of the Australians at Lord's against England.[120]

The 'little trickiness' seems to have gone by the time Surrey batted, as they racked up 424 and went on to win by an innings and 115 runs. *Cricket* did not insult its readers by pointing out the common factor in the two demolition jobs. Among many spectacular performances, this was towards the top and was still fresh in the mind of Corœbus of the *Morning Advertiser* some sixteen years later when he penned his obituary appreciation:

Richardson fizzed off the pitch and even at his pace broke back as much as any slow bowler would have done. No wonder the Notts batsmen failed. I never saw any bowling so horribly difficult to play. [121]

In selecting Richardson as one of the Five Cricketers of the Season, *Wisden* was less hyperbolic, less romantic, less poetic than Cardus was subsequently to be, but, in its prosaic, traditional way, no less complimentary:

His greatest feats last summer were certainly performed in the England matches at Lord's and Manchester. On the last day at Old Trafford, he bowled unchanged for three hours and nearly won a match in which England had followed on against a majority of 181 runs. The characteristics of Richardson's bowling are too well known to require detailed description. It is generally agreed that no bowler, with the same tremendous speed, has ever possessed such a break from the off. Personally no professional cricketer in England enjoys greater popularity with the general public and among his brother players.[122]

Evidence from those who played with him confirms the truth of that last sentence, though he was not exactly flavour of the month of August with the Surrey committee. The players' 'strike' – or maybe lockout – of August 1896 in which Richardson, along with his county team mates Abel, Hayward and Lohmann and Nottinghamshire's William Gunn, was involved has been dealt with in some detail from both sides in my earlier biographies of Charles Alcock and George Lohmann.[123] The *Surrey Independent* took a considered, middle-of-the-road view that the professionals undoubtedly had a case, but that the timing and approach could be criticised:

The question that has been agitating the minds of the cricket world this week has been the 'great strike' of the professionals – Abel, Gunn, Richardson, Hayward and Lohmann and varied are the views that have been expressed in the London press on the matter, but most agree with the action of the Surrey County Committee in refusing to comply with the professionals' *demand* for £20 and expenses in the last great

120   *Cricket* 6 August 1896
121   reproduced in *Mitcham Advertiser* 12 July 1912
122   1897 p xlvii
123   *The Father of Modern Sport* pp 197-209; *George Lohmann, Pioneer Professional* pp 211-229

test match, instead of £10 as hitherto. Whilst not denying that the five named pros are well worth the extra money the demand appears to have been ill-timed and the words used in making the request were such as to certainly not ensure respectful consideration of the proposal.

But the ventilation of the comparatively poor pay received by the professionals for their services in such an important game as England v Australia when every nerve has to be strained to the utmost, will undoubtedly do some good. Much has been written as to the greatest cricketer that ever lived – Dr W.G.Grace – receiving £10 for expenses for the match and the attacks on the G.O.M. of cricket have been numerous, a morning contemporary being especially bitter, but I maintain that the sum is none too great for a journey to and from Gloucestershire, hotel and other expenses of a three day stay in town.

The real grievance lies in the fact that the pros do not receive remuneration equal to what their services demand and especially considering what each member of the Australian team will carry away, and that this may be remedied in future is the wish of every sportsman. The action of Abel, Hayward and Richardson in placing themselves in the hands of the Surrey executive is to be commended, and the courteous letter Lohmann has since written to them shows he appreciates their kindness to him. Gunn, too, is only anxious to see this vexed question more fairly dealt with.

Turning to the great match itself, it is a matter of satisfaction that the Old Country has won the rubber.[124] The superb bowling of Hearne and Peel will long be remembered – and none more so than by the Australians themselves – while the batting of Abel and the stand on the first day by Jackson and Grace did much to place England in the premier position. When W.G. shunted Richardson for Peel in the second innings there were many cavillings, but the wisdom of the veteran cricketer was exemplified by the astonishing result.[125]

Despite Lohmann's subsequent enforced apology and withdrawal of the word 'demand', it does not seem out of place and was a normal, negotiating word for the infant trade unions of the late nineteenth century. In context, it seems no more provocative than its use in the second line of the third paragraph of the above extract though admittedly it may have seemed offensive to the Surrey committee who had little to do with trade unions and still subscribed to the concept of deference – which was fine for those being deferred to, perhaps less so, though apparently acceptable, for those doing the deferring.

Notwithstanding his match-winning performance at Lord's and his monumental single-handed effort at Old Trafford, Richardson was scarcely used in the Oval Test match, bowling five overs in the first innings and just one in the second. Admittedly the pitch was damp after rain on the first day and perhaps more suited to the bowling of Peel and Hearne, and

---

124   Not the 'Ashes' which seems to have had little significance at the time.
125   *Surrey Independent* 16 August 1896

Australia's 44 all out is, as the newspaper suggests, sufficient vindication of Grace's choice of bowlers; but one wonders whether there was not an element of recrimination because of events earlier in the week.

There had been controversy of a different kind earlier in the summer when the reaction to what *Cricket* described as an epidemic of 'half-way fast bowling' resulted in Albert Trott being taken off at the request of the MCC Secretary. The magazine commented:

> It has been said that if fast bowlers are not allowed to bowl as they please in first-class cricket the game becomes a farce but already there have been occasions in first-class cricket when the captains have mutually agreed not to put on their fast bowlers because of the danger.

'Half-way fast bowling' was never part of Richardson's armoury, but with Ernest Jones around, allegedly putting the ball through W.G's beard[126] and all-rounder Albert Trott, nursing a grudge against the Australian selectors,[127] fast bowling was in the news. There were to be few occasions in the history of the game when it was not.

Notwithstanding the different approaches, *Cricket* in its summary of the season put Richardson ahead of Jones:

> Frequently, too, wickets were so fiery that batsmen could not touch fast bowling, and during this period, Jones and Richardson had a beanfeast...Richardson's bowling was magnificent. In my opinion, he is the greatest bowler in the world today.[128]

Despite that, Surrey relinquished the Championship title to Yorkshire.

Over the years there have been several claimants to the title of 'the greatest bowler in the world' and the debate remains unresolved, despite many hours of debate in public bars and elsewhere. When asked to suggest a title for what eventually became *Fred: Portrait of a Fast Bowler*, the subject of John Arlott's biography, the author recalls, with typical modesty

> rolled it off the tongue, pat as if rehearsed – 'T' Definitive Volume of t'Finest Fast Bowler that Ever Drew Breath'[129]

Sydney Barnes, like Trueman, a man aware of his own standing in the bowling hierarchy, reckoned Richardson was the only one that bore comparison with him[130] and the subsequent claims of Larwood, Tyson, Lillee and the great Caribbean combinations of the late twentieth century cannot be disregarded. But it can safely be said that Richardson is up there with the best and perhaps unique in sustaining his pace for a day, a match, and a season or four.

It came as no surprise that, as a result of yet another outstanding season,

126   Whimpress *Ernie Jones* p 21
127   Having missed selection for the tour, he had financed his own trip from Australia to England and secured a place on the MCC groundstaff – *Who's Who of Cricketers* p 1025 [1984 edition]
128   *Cricket* 17 September 1896
129   pp 183-184
130   *Barker* Ten Great Bowlers p 179

Wisden named him along with Syd Gregory, A.F.A.Lilley, K.S.Ranjitsinhji and Hugh Trumble, as one of its *Five Cricketers of the Season.* He had no chance of a nomination in any of the previous four seasons, the equivalent awards going to batsmen (twice), allrounders, and W.G.Grace.

In its customary manner *Wisden* recounted the details of Tom's career up to the end of 1896, emphasising his position in being currently 'the first of English bowlers'. The writer mentioned that at first Richardson was thought to have thrown a great deal but that now there was no question as to the purity of his action.[131]

---

131   1897 p xlvii

Chapter Seven
1897...Jubilee and Millennium

The millennial year
Rushes on to our view and eternity's here.

Charles Wesley 1707-88

At the beginning of the year, *Cricket* undertook a statistical exercise on the figures of the leading bowlers over the previous ten years, 1887-1896, producing a fairly crude, but not entirely meaningless, 'figure of merit' by adding average runs per wicket to average overs per wicket. The magazine was quick to admit the limitations of the method.

> Too great a reliance upon statistics is ridiculous, but averages have this value: they give some approximate idea of the work done by a player and how it compares with that of his rivals. And they count for more in estimating the real greatness of a player when they are spread over a series of years than when they merely represent the work of one year.[132]

With that caveat and also allowing for the fact that the statistics have been refined over the years, Richardson is firmly in second place behind 'The Terror' Turner, behind him and a couple of others on average, but well ahead of all but one on strike-rate.

	Runs/Wkt	Overs/Wkt	'Figure of Merit'
C.T.B.Turner	12.30	7.12	19.42
T.Richardson	14.42	5.89	20.31
T.R.McKibbin	14.26	6.40	20.66
G.A.Lohmann	13.53	7.61	21.14
A.Mold	14.65	7.11	21.76
F.G.Bull	17.64	4.88	22.52
J.Briggs	14.45	8.33	22.78
E.Jones	16.03	7.17	23.20

Tom began 1897 as he had finished 1896 with a hatful of wickets as Leicestershire found him almost unplayable, his match figures being 12 for 105, six in each innings:

> The rest did very little, while in the second innings, no one could play Richardson who began the season with a very fine analysis. Surrey had the easiest of victories but a good many friends of the county must feel that it would have been a little more satisfactory if, besides Richardson and Hayward, more of the other bowlers had shown promise of taking wickets during the season.[133]

---

132   *Cricket* 28 January 1897
133   *Cricket* 6 May 1897

In the return match the following month, it was even easier. The match was finished in a day - one of only five in the Club's history - as 'Richardson again had a wonderful record.'[134] He and Hayward bowled through both innings as Leicestershire were twice dismissed for 35 and Richardson returned 12-8-6-5 and 12-6-14-7.

By 18 June, he was through 100 wickets, three days earlier than the previous season, but behind J.T.Hearne who reached the benchmark on 12 June. They were the only two members of the Players side which met the Gentlemen at The Oval, who had never scored a first-class century, but they had made their contribution in other ways. By 15 July Richardson had taken 125, Hearne 119: the amateurs between them had taken 101. No doubt who did the bowling during the amateur-professional divide. Ironically, neither starred in the match, but with just a few runs required to win the match in the fourth innings, Richardson was allowed to open the batting and made 27 not out from 31 while two wickets fell at the other end.

The following week in the Lord's version of the same fixture, it was back to normal, batting at No.11, ten wickets in the match, eight bowled, two lbw in a win by 78 runs. Players were dominant now leading *Cricket* to report almost apologetically

> .. despite the failures of so many great players the Gentlemen made a splendid fight.[135]

He did not need to move his kit from Lord's, Surrey's next match being there; nor was there any dip in his form as he added another thirteen to the fourth column in an eight-wicket victory. There can be little doubt about Richardson's superiority at this stage of his career and Surrey were surprised that anyone else, however distinguished, could hold a different opinion.

> Mr C.B.FRY in a recently published article expresses an opinion that Lockwood in his best form is a more difficult bowler than Richardson. This will be news to the Surrey committee and the Surrey eleven, although if the remark had been made three or four years ago, it would perhaps have met with approval.[136]

Certainly the statistics over those years would have demonstrated the superiority of Richardson's record over Lockwood's; but one can see where Fry is coming from. Like his friend and colleague, Ranjitsinhji, he could appreciate Lockwood's greater variety, but would have acknowledged Richardson's greater consistency.

The match against Essex at Leyton was an eventful one and was both started and finished by Richardson:

> From the beginning of the game, the wicket was just a little tricky - just tricky enough to give experienced bowlers like Richardson and

---

134   *Cricket* 17 June 1897
135   *Cricket* 15 July 1897
136   *Cricket* 22 July 1897

Hayward a great advantage.

The very beginning of the match was disastrous and ominous for Essex, Carpenter being bowled neck and crop with the first ball of the innings by Richardson... one or two balls from Richardson acted very queerly, and the batsmen were not able to inspire confidence in their success.

In the end, Surrey needed only ten to win: as in the Gentlemen v Players match earlier in the season, Richardson was allowed to open the innings. He did the job, making all ten and completing the victory set up earlier by his seven for 60 in the first innings.

Then, at Beckenham

Almost from the beginning of this match it was seen that runs would only be made with the greatest of difficulty and that some pluck would be required to stand up against the fast bowlers. Under these circumstances it is not surprising that Richardson was in clover, and that Kent were outclassed.

... if ever there was a certainty in cricket, it was certain that runs could not be made against Richardson and Hayward.

Richardson's 27.3-11-49-8 and 16.5-5-53-6 was the principal contributory factor to a win by 156 runs in under two days.

Then came what *Cricket* styled THE GREAT COUNTY MATCH OF 1897, against Lancashire at The Oval and likely to determine the County Championship. In fact, it didn't. Surrey won the match by six wickets, but the remainder of the season's results went Lancashire's way. They won the Championship for the first time.

Although it was not absolutely certain that the result of this match would determine which side would be Champion County for the ensuing year, there can be no question that the meeting of the two counties was considered by most people as a sort of final tie ... after lunch a most remarkable change came over the game. Sugg increased his score by 7 – he was 50 not out at lunch time – and was then bowled by Richardson, after which the end came with surprising suddenness. Lees and Richardson were the bowlers, the former taking three wickets after lunch for four runs in five overs, and the latter three for ten runs in the same number of overs.[137]

Surrey lost by 66 runs at Taunton, but Richardson remained top of the tree both in his home county and in England:

Richardson is the bright particular star among English bowlers at present; no amount of work seems to tire him, and his performances for Surrey were simply wonderful. Lees backed him up well and worked hard to fill the void left by Lohmann.[138]

137   *Cricket* 26 August 1897
138   *Cricket* 9 September 1897

For Surrey alone, Richardson had taken 238 wickets in 1,398 overs: Hayward 91 in 713.1, Lees 75 in 661.2, Brockwell 37 in 434.1. It was indicative of a workload which, coupled with what he had to get through on the coming winter's tour of Australia, was to precipitate a decline in his effectiveness. He continued to take wickets and plenty of them, but no longer at the rate of over two hundred a year.

But his season was not over. The Hastings Festival followed and the wickets continued to come, seven for 47 for the South against the North at Hastings, six for 98 and seven for 63 for the Players against the Gentlemen.

It brought his tally for the season to 273 and for four seasons to 1,005 (1,073 if the 1894/95 tour of Australia is included), an achievement to which no other fast bowler has come close, though leg-break and googly bowler 'Tich' Freeman had 1,122 in his record-breaking season and the three subsequent ones.[139]

> Richardson's standing in the cricketing firmament was at its highest and he was the benchmark against which others were measured. Pelham Warner on tour on the United States said in one of his speeches

> It has been said by the admirers of Mr King that on his day he is, with the exception of the famous Tom Richardson, the greatest bowler in the world; I see no reason to cavil at the verdict.[140]

In the full heat of the statistical explosion of the 1890s, F.S.Ashley-Cooper in SOME STATISTICS OF THE SEASON pointed out that

> Tom Richardson bowled in 59 innings and only in two of the 59 did his efforts go unrewarded.[141]

He took his 200th wicket of the season on 13 August at Leyton on his way to a season's total of 273. He had 15 wickets in a match on three occasions and took wickets in all of the thirty matches in which he bowled.

Albert Craig updated his sketch of 'Thomas Richardson':

> unlike George Lohmann, this crack fast bowler is a Surreyite by birth, which is a superior characteristic to all 'qualifying fakements' so frequently resorted to. On 11th of August 1870, the year remarkable for the conclusion of the Franco-German war, Tom Richardson disturbed the quiet serenity of Byfleet by the initial usage of his lungs. Since acquiring the knowledge of how to use a cricket ball, he has disturbed a great number of wickets.[142]

Such was Craig's slightly Quixotic interpretation of Richardson's very early days. *Wisden* yet again highlighted the fact that Richardson was now head and shoulders above any other bowler:

> They, of course, possessed in Richardson, far and away the best bowler in the country, but it was a little disquieting to supporters of

---

139   *Wisden* 2012 pp 1262-3
140   *Cricket* 25 November 1897
141   *Cricket* 18 December 1897
142   *Captain of the Crowd* p 88

the county to see how much depended on one man. Happily the great fast bowler was in perfect health all through the summer, and did not meet with a mishap of any kind. Had he been laid aside at any time by illness or accident, Surrey would have suffered to a far greater extent than Lancashire did in August from the breakdown of Mold. The absence of George Lohmann threw a greater responsibility than ever upon Richardson, but he rose to the occasion in a wonderful way and took in county matches alone 238 wickets for something over fourteen runs each. Just at the start of the season he was scarcely himself, and fears were expressed that he was losing his spin. All ideas of this kind, however, soon proved to be erroneous. Once in form, Richardson remained at his best till the season was over, the days being very few upon which he did not come out with a good average. Considering his tremendous pace, his capacity for hard work was scarcely less remarkable than his skill. He bowled in every innings played against Surrey during the season in county matches, and when he had to be taken off, the side never seemed quite happy till he was on again. Among all his fine performances, there was perhaps nothing better than his effort in the final stage of the match against Middlesex at the Oval. With Lees and Hayward to help him, he got Middlesex out on a fairly good wicket for 88, and it is no exaggeration to say, that in the course of two hours he scarcely bowled a bad ball. A famous member of the beaten side said afterwards, that he had scarcely thought it possible for Richardson to keep up his great pace for such a length of time, in combination with great accuracy. There is no need here to go into details of what Richardson did for Surrey last season, but one can say with truth that, on hard wickets, he was so much superior to all his rivals.[143]

Fifteen years later, at the end of his life, *The Times* was able to put the period in its historical context:

> ... he went into the front rank, and for five seasons he remained at his very best, Indeed no fast bowler in modern days was ever so consistently successful as he was from 1893 to 1897 inclusive. Considering the excellence of the grounds on which he had to bowl, his achievements were remarkable.[144]

---

143   *Wisden* 1898 pp23-24
144   4 July 1912

Scorebook – Thames Ditton v Addlestone, 1897: Tom 7 – 37.
[Surrey History Centre and Thames Ditton Cricket Club]

Chapter Eight
Australia 1897/98

In May 1897 it was announced that A.E.Stoddart would again lead a team to Australia as guests of the Melbourne Cricket Club and the Sydney ground trustees. Richardson was an automatic choice for the tour, but he made less of an impression than he had three years earlier.

The tour was far less successful both for the team and for Richardson than the previous one in 1894/95. Still under 28, the age at which conventionally fast bowlers reach their peak, there was no way he could continue indefinitely to bowl at his pace and for the long periods to which he had been accustomed. The heat and the hard Australian pitches took their toll. In first-class matches he took 54 wickets against 68, in the Tests 22 against 32 both at a much higher average. England lost the series 4-1; compared with a 3-2 victory three years earlier. The difference was not unrelated to the difference in Richardson's form.

> I never imagined that I would celebrate winning the Ashes in Australia with half-an-hour's sleep in the back of the SCG pavilion. But then, I have bowled 213 overs in this series, which is a figure I have never even approached before.

That was Jimmy Anderson at the conclusion of the 2010/11 Test series.[145] For a modern cricketer that is on the high side. Richardson bowled 255 overs in the Tests; three years earlier it was 291. On each occasion he bowled over 500 in all first-class matches as well as a few in the less serious up-country matches and those against odds. The time span was slightly longer, but modern cricketers have the advantage of expert medical attention and teams of fitness advisers and physiotherapists, which were not available in the late nineteenth century.

The series began well enough. Stoddart was mourning the loss of his mother and MacLaren took over the captaincy. Ranjitsinhji scored a century on his first Test appearance in Australia, having already done so on his first appearance in England and MacLaren also registered a hundred on his first Test as captain. England ran up 551 and Australia followed on more than three hundred behind. Their second innings was better, thanks in part to some untypically erratic bowling by Richardson, occasioned possibly by increasing weight, possibly by incipient rheumatism or maybe a combination of both, as well as impending burnout, the effect on his body caused by the equivalent of just over 7,500 five-ball overs of fast bowling in the past five years. However, England's first innings total had been sufficient. Time was not an issue – these were timeless Tests – and they knocked off the handful of runs required to win by nine wickets.

---

145   *Sunday Telegraph* 9 January 2011

It was a good win, but a false dawn. 'Felix' in *The Australasian* was among the first to notice the beginnings of decline:

> I fancy Richardson is putting on flesh a bit on this trip, in spite of his passion for long walks, and is not quite as fit as on his first visit. I never saw him bowl so erratically as in the second innings at Sydney – wides, no balls, head balls, and then a succession of maiden overs that kept the batsmen hard on the defensive all the while. Charlie McLeod got two of the head balls, one the now historic no-ball[146] that pitched on top of his wicket, while the other would have pitched on his ear had he not ducked. Jack Lyons got one on the chest – that needed a plaster later on – and had he stepped away from it, it would have gone very close to the wicket, and the bowler, I fancy, appealed for l.b.w. One of his wides was a most awful wide – quite ten feet off the wicket.[147]

Between the First and Second Tests, in the few days spanning Christmas and New Year, there was the opportunity for relaxation in and around the gold rush town of Bendigo, though one incident related by John Lazenby, grandson of one of Richardson's team-mates, Jack Mason, in a book based on his grandfather's diaries, was anything but relaxing. He describes the following encounter with one of the Antipodes' less attractive denizens when hunting in the Gippsland bush:

> when a large black snake suddenly reared its head from the very place in which he was about to plant his size 11 boot. The serpent was all of 5 feet 6 inches long, big enough to have swallowed little Johnny Briggs whole, and to turn Richardson's blood to ice on the spot, but before it could lock its eyes on to his, the Surrey crack had taken aim and, with deadly precision, killed the reptile stone dead with a single shot. The skin would return to England with him as a trophy to show his county teammates and a reminder of his brush with death. Those who had been with him in the bush that day remembered how the barrel of the gun rocked in the giant's hand before the bullet found its mark.[148]

In the New Year Test at Melbourne, Australia came back with 520 and a victory by an innings and 55 runs. On the first day

> The two bowlers, Richardson and Hearne, on whom the success of England was supposed chiefly to depend, did not take a wicket between them

and on the second

> Richardson, Hearne and Hirst had about a hundred runs hit off them for only a wicket each, which was indeed a sad experience.[149]

In his diary of the tour, Richardson describes the pitch as 'very crumbly', but acknowledges the 'very fine performance' of the Australians.[150]

146　McLeod was run out by Storer when he left his crease after being bowled by a no-ball. His deafness prevented him from hearing the umpire's call.
147　Reproduced in *Cricket* 24 February 1898
148　*Test of Time* pp 149-150
149　*Cricket* 24 February 1898
150　5 January 1898

The Third Test at Adelaide was no better – another innings defeat and Australia well past 200 with only one wicket down.

> Richardson, who at last was fortunate enough to get a wicket...[151]

This time, Richardson is less gracious in defeat. He acknowledges Australia's superiority, but is privately critical of the umpiring:

> There is no doubt they played far superior cricket all round yet we had to fight against bad decisions of which we had more than our share and I think on several occasions it was simply disgraceful.

The only consolation from the Fourth Test was that England managed to avoid defeat by an innings, but it was eight wickets as a youthful Clem Hill's 188 saw Australia to a total of 323, low in the context of the series but a sufficient basis for a win by a significant margin. Hearne had six for 98, Richardson a modest two for 102 in 26 overs. Hill apparently relished taking on quick bowling; his century followed three consecutive half-centuries and this was very probably the occasion on which Tom is alleged to have remarked to him:

> You make me feel I took up fast bowling for your benefit.[152]

The series was now decided. Richardson had a modicum of revenge on Hill in the final Test at Sydney, bowling him twice for eight and two. The one who would 'live in history as perhaps the finest of all fast bowlers'[153] signed off his Test career with his best figures of 8-94, enabling England to take a first-innings lead of 96 and, for a while it looked as though the trend of the series might be bucked, but a below-par batting performance in the second innings followed by Darling's 160 returned matters to normal. Jack Fingleton reckons that this must have been one of the greatest innings of all time as Richardson was forced to have three men in the outfield.[154] Richardson took his wicket eventually, his 88th and last in Test cricket; but by then the match and Richardson's Test career were as good as over.

Richardson's first-innings figures are the third-best figures for bowling in a Test at the SCG after Lohmann's two 'eight-for's on his 1886/87 and 1891/92 tours.

His indifferent form returned in the state match against Victoria, but he did redeem himself in the second innings with five for 35 after two for 104 in the first.

> Except for 59 by H.Stuckey, who is in fine form this season, and 39 by Trott, the bowling for a change had mastery of the batting. Richardson was again expensive.

> ...The wicket had been upset by rain, with the result that when Victoria went in again with a lead of 50, Richardson was at last able to do

---

151   19 January 1898
152   Website: *Legside Filth*
153   *Wisden* Obituary 1913 p 195
154   *The Immortal Victor Trumper* p 111

*Portraits of A.E.Stoddart's team which sailed on the SS Ormuz
to Australia for the 1897/98 tour.
[Cricket Philatelic Society]*

himself full justice.[155]

Despite his mediocre form in a series of mediocre results, he was the leading wicket-taker on the trip with 54 – albeit at an average of almost thirty – and 65 in all matches, ahead of Hearne with 44 and 61.

There was one achievement in Australia which had nothing to do with his bowling. Twice, at his customary batting position of No.11, he improved on his career-best Test batting, 24 not out in the First Test in Sydney, sharing a tenth-wicket partnership of 74 in half an hour with Ranjitsinhji who let him down by getting out for 175, then eclipsed that with 25 in the Third at Adelaide.

The *Daily Telegraph*, wise after the event, described Stoddart's team as 'the team of all the failures'. *Cricket* did not disagree but pointed to its late summer prescience the previous year.

> That is not very far wrong and it is at least certain that MacLaren is the only member of the team who has increased his reputation....

> When Mr Stoddart's team was practically complete last August, the following remarks appeared in Gossip: "The bowling is still very weak,

---

155   *Cricket* 31 August 1898

and although bowling averages may not be a wholly satisfactory test of ability a glance at the *Sportsman* list of last Monday is calculated to make Englishmen thoughtful. Richardson is *fourth* with an average of 16.10, Hearne *tenth* with 18.42, Hayward *fifteenth* with 19.30; the next in the list is *Hirst* who is no nearer the top than *twenty-sixth*, Wainwright is *thirty-second* and Mr Mason *thirty-fifth*. In other words, only one of the bowlers is in the first nine, and only two are in the first twenty-five. To use a colloquial expression: 'What price this?' "[156]

There were the expected inquests.

In an article on the 'Differences between English and Australian cricket' Mr MacLaren, in the *London Review* gives various reasons for the failure of the Englishmen during their recent tour. They may be briefly summarised as follows:-

1. Climatic influences. Heat; kills bowlers, batsman get out from pure exhaustion. Prevents sleep at night.
2. Tremendous glare. Difficult to judge a high catch.
3. Extraordinary pace of wickets. Inability of man to alter strokes, which were useful at home; not quick enough for late cut or hook stroke.
4. Hot winds. Knock our bowlers out.
5. Playing against Local Eighteen on a matting wicket after a "test" match. Ball comes above your head, and when you return to turf wickets you feel strange.
6. Accidents; illness; hard work.[157]

Whingeing Poms? Other English teams had faced similar conditions and had done better. The real reasons perhaps owed more to the fact that, beginning with the 1891/92 tour, interest in cricket in Australia had begun to revive and the interest raised by the Sheffield Shield, and then by the 1894/95 tour, had generated the momentum which had led to an improvement in standards. The situation was to change very little throughout the following century.

Rather more philosophically, Ranjitsinhji commented:

Cricketers of exceptional merit, and well-known authorities on the game, have often endeavoured to find out what is "form" and how it deteriorates and why it often does not come up to expectations. But although they have been able to ascertain the first two, they have never been satisfactorily able to give a true and reasonable explanation for the latter. Where better men than I have failed, I am not too proud to acknowledge my own total inability to explain the non-recovery of form of my comrades, who, with myself, on our present tour, tried hard and did our best to uphold the best traditions of English cricket – with but imperfect success...

... The great misfortune to the team was the rheumatism which, at times, affected Tom Richardson's right arm. Everyone in Australia is

156   24 February 1898
157   *Cricket* 18 May 1898

aware of the important part he played in all the games during Stoddart's tour of 1894-5. His comparative failure on this tour was the greatest disappointment to us, and affected our position most seriously.[158]

'Felix' had commented on the increasing weight but was perhaps not aware of the rheumatism. Richardson himself was painfully aware that his contribution had fallen short of the high standards established on the previous tour. Interviewed for *The Boy's Own Paper*, before some airbrushed in comments on the importance of cricket to the Empire, he says, in reply to a question about playing cricket twelve months a year:

> My own experience is against it. The strain is so great that it is a mistake to play all year round.[159]

He kept a diary on this tour, a couple of extracts from which are given earlier. It was recently auctioned at Christie's, the estimated price £10-15,000, rather outside the resources of the ACS. It is leather-backed and contains the original pencil. Although it starts cheerfully enough, commending the play of Clem Hill in the match against South Australia it peters out at the end of January in the middle of the Fourth Test in which Richardson comments favourably on Hill's innings to the end of the first day:

> ... Hill's 182 not out ..one could not speak too highly, he having played by far the best innings I have ever seen.[160]

There are no more entries, significant perhaps in that its discontinuation reflects Richardson's utter exhaustion by this stage of the tour.

It is not only cricket, however. Colour is added by the relation of a number of off-the-field incidents:

> ...went to hear concert at Town Hall which was very good but a bit too classic for us.[161]

> On arriving at Brisbane at 10:30 it was something dreadful, there being a large and disorderly crowd in which Mr Stoddart got his watch stolen.[162]

> went to the convict station St Helena and saw some very rough looking customers.[163]

According to J.T.Hearne's description, these were striking sheep shearers convicted of shed burning. Hearne's diary is a fuller – or, at least, more accessible – account of the tour in both its cricketing and non-cricketing aspects and was serialised in *The Cricketer* in 1982. It is consistent with the Richardson version and the Jack Mason biography in the anecdotes about Stoddart's watch being stolen in Brisbane and about the snake, although in the case of the latter it does add:

---

158   *With Stoddart's Team in Australia* – quoted in *Cricket* 1 September 1898
159   *The Boy's Own Paper* 1899: pp651-2
160   29 January 1898
161   18 November 1897
162   24 November 1897
163   28 November 1887

Poor Tom Rich got a rare fright from one of the snakes before he shot it. I may say we were all walking in a most careless and reckless manner when he (Tom) came acoss this brute within a foot of him and then he only saw it just as it shot up its head ready to strike. He says he cannot describe his feelings at that moment. However, he got back a few yards and gave him both barrels ... (Black snake most deadly – kills in two hours of bite)[164]

There seems to have been a harmony between the players on the tour, at least initially. It is perhaps not without significance that, like Richardson's, the diary peters out in January, suggesting a bit of *weltschmertz* with a long tour, at a time when the wheels were beginning to come off; but before that there are descriptions of seasickness on the outward voyage, the wearying journeys, the draining effects of the heat, the mosquitoes, the varying quality of the hotels, the games of poker and solo whist and the hostility and ignorance of Australian barrackers:

Farce of a day – in and out about six times for showers. Spectators very raw about it. Wanted us to get wet through for their benefit.[165]

In Toowoomba they seem to have had not too happy a time:

Public seem quite ignorant of the game here too. Putting up at Queen's Head hotel

...Two in a room, poor beds. Myriads of mosquitoes as big as butterflies, worst hotel we have been in and waitresses most unobliging.[166]

None the less, he was impressed with the Australian enthusiasm for the game. In Sydney, for instance, while the tourists are playing New South Wales,

People seem highly enthusiastic on the game here. Scoreboards at different parts of city, giving account of game in progress. Thousands of people watching – almost stop traffic, folks unable to get to the ground.[167]

As the leading bowlers on the tour, Hearne and Richardson seem to have developed a bond, the kind that perhaps springs from rivalry. Even in the same side bowlers compete with one another, usually on friendly terms, for wickets and the Surrey-Middlesex divide is a long-standing one. Early in the diary Hearne mentions an argument about socialism he had with 'Tom',[168] suggesting that there was some thinking 'outside the box' and serious conversations about matters other than cricket. Hearne continued to play first-class cricket for a further quarter of a century, but would not

---

164   *Cricketer* January 1983 p 35
165   *Cricketer* August 1982 p 40. There was a suspicion that the game was wrapped up early to allow the team to travel to Melbourne in time for the Melbourne Cup.
166   *Cricketer* November 1982 p 55
167   *Cricketer* September 1982 p 27
168   *Cricketer* May 1982 p 28 – possibly Hayward, but an editorial note suggests more probably Richardson.

team up again in the same England side as his fast-bowling colleague for whom this tour marked the beginning of a gradual decline.

Richardson was never to play for England again. In fourteen Test matches he had distinguished himself with eleven five-wicket innings and four

ten-wicket matches. He remains the only English bowler to achieve the latter; Briggs and Lohmann have three to their credit, no one else more than two.

A Tom Richardson Miniature donated to Surrey County Cricket Club 'in memory of his visit to Australia'.

The Inscription on the back reads "To Tom Richardson in memory of his visit to Australia from C. Roberts 17/2/1898".

[Surrey County Cricket Club Museum]

Chapter Nine
Fin-de-Siècle

1898

After his return from Australia, Tom was never the same player again. Fast bowlers, it is said, reach their peak about the age of 28. Richardson's zenith was a little before that. The plateau at which he was at his very best had lasted four years, a sharp incline to reach it, a tour of Australia in its midst and a gradual decline beginning with his second tour of Australia.

The tour had taken its toll – on everyone. The amateurs, however, had the luxury of being able to take a couple of weeks off. Not so the professionals. They had a living to earn.

> Of the amateur members of Mr Stoddart's team not one has yet taken part in first-class cricket this year. Nearly all the professionals have begun the season well especially Hayward, Storer and J.T.Hearne. Richardson did wonderfully well at first but received a slight shock in the Essex match.[169]

Three years earlier, a successful tour of Australia had been followed by a record-breaking wicket-taking season. A less successful tour was followed by a less successful season in which Richardson took 'only' 161 wickets at an average at 19.54, acceptable enough, but below the high standards of earlier seasons. He began with 25.4-13-32-6 for C.I.Thornton's England XI against Cambridge University at Fenner's. Three for 108 and two for 53 against Essex was nearer the norm for that season, though he still managed twelve five-wicket innings and four ten-wicket matches.

Surrey had a slow start to the season, accelerated towards the end, but it was not enough to give them a Championship placing higher than fourth.

Longfellow's *Psalm of Life* provided the framework and the metre for an optimistic parody:

> Tell me not in mournful numbers
> "Surrey is a rotten team
> For its bowling talent slumbers
> And the batsmen sleepy seem!"

> Wait till we begin in earnest.
> With our eyes set on the goal!
> When thou, Tom, to form returnest
> When thou dost begin to bowl!
> ...

---

169   *Cricket* 19 May 1898

Lives of great teams all remind us
We may yet far upwards climb
And, in autumn, leave behind us
Rivals knocked clean out on time.
       Longfellow (up-to-date)[170]

The weather that summer was not the greatest.

With rain day after day, with wintry temperatures, with matches abandoned everywhere as drawn. With such happenings as 38 runs for three wickets being the full score of a game in which play was attempted on all three days.[171]

After a less than impressive start to the season (at least by the standards he had set over the previous four seasons), occasioned no doubt by the after-effects of the winter tour, Tom's form began to pick up. Against Oxford University

Richardson bowled better than he has done for some time.[172]

His three for 60 and five for 41 helped Surrey to a victory by an innings and three runs. Then the following week, Somerset were beaten by nine wickets, Richardson's contribution being 19.2-2-68-7 and 41-9-117-5:

Richardson bowled so well that memories of his former great successes were revived.[173]

At Chesterfield, he took the first three wickets - all bowled – and followed that with a ten-wicket match against Hampshire; then, the third hat-trick of his career, against Sussex in George Bean's benefit match:

In their second innings, the home team began fairly well, but when Richardson got rid of Mr Brann, Mr Murdoch and Mr Newham with successive balls, the rot set in.[174]

Against Leicestershire Richardson bowled very well[175] and the earlier heavy defeat by Yorkshire was amply avenged in the return fixture at The Oval as the visitors responded to Surrey's 536 with 78 and 186.

Lockwood and Richardson were in irresistible form.

… and Waterloo provided the framework for a bit more late nineteenth-century doggerel.

THE BATTLE OF THE OVAL
It was a summer evening
When Apted's work was done:
And he before the scoring box
Was sitting in the sun;
And by him squatted on the green

---

170   *Cricket* 16 June 1898
171   *Cricket* 23 June 1898
172   *Cricket* 23 June 1898
173   *Cricket* 30 June 1898
174   *Cricket* 14 July 1898
175   *Cricket* 21 July 1898

A youngster and a critic keen.
...
"Now tell us how the Tykes got out,"
The anxious youngster cries:
And then the critic keen looked up
A tear in both his eyes;
"Now tell us all about the rot
And of the licking Yorkshire got."

" 'Twas Tom and Lockwood," Apted cried
"That put the Tykes to rout;
But why they did on such a pitch,
I cannot well make out
But everybody said," quoth he
"That 'twas a famous victory."[176]

Then Tom acquired a new partner in Ernest Hayes, a bowler of a quite different style.

The two bowlers who had a hand in this collapse were Richardson and Hayes. The former kept an excellent length and bowled with great judgment. The latter, with his notional breaks from the leg, tied up the batsmen in the most astonishing manner.[177]

Richardson had the advantage of being a member of a side that was strong in batting.

In the Sussex match at the Oval, the Surrey team were disposed of in their second innings for less than 300, for the first time this season in a completed innings.[178]

Conversely, against Somerset at Taunton, he was obliged to carry the bowling almost single-handed:

Lockwood returned to London with an arm injury...the whole brunt of the attack fell on Richardson who worked exceedingly hard with much success.[179]

In an innings of 139.3 overs spread unevenly between eight bowlers, he had 53.3-14-164-7. There followed a major performance in the last Championship match of the season against Warwickshire at The Oval. First he contributed 28 to a tenth-wicket partnership with Harry Wood, taking the total from 541 to 609, then twice demolished the visitors with 27-4-55-7 and 19-8-28-8, finishing the innings with his second hat-trick of the season. Abel and Brockwell's opening partnership exceeded the combined total of both Warwickshire innings. It was a satisfactory end to a season with a less than satisfactory beginning.

It was perhaps the beginning of the Richardson twilight but it was certainly not without its last gleaming. In the Hastings festival, for A.E.Stoddart's

176   *Cricket* 11 August 1898
177   *Cricket* 18 August 1898
178   *Cricket* 18 August 1898
179   *Cricket* 1 September 1898

*Cartoon of
Tom Richardson in
rare batting mode.
[Harmsworth Magazine:
Volume 1, 1898/99]*

XI against The Rest he took out MacLaren, Grace and Jessop, and for a Surrey and Sussex XI against The Rest in his eight for 52, his victims were MacLaren, Grace, Storer, Jessop, Board, Hirst, Briggs and Rhodes. He finished 22nd in the first-class averages[180] and despite his relatively modest season, his total of 161 wickets was second only to J.T.Hearne's 222.

Cricket summed up Surrey's season.

> At the beginning of the year it was feared that Surrey would be terribly weak in bowling, for Richardson, after a few successes on difficult wickets, lost his pace and was no longer the Richardson of last year. There seemed no one to take his place, for he had been head and shoulders above the other bowlers. Happily Lockwood again came into the team, and from first to last bowled in splendid form, and as Richardson occasionally came out with a good analysis, it was seldom that the attack was found wanting.[181]

Wisden, while commenting on Lockwood's 'restoration', drew the inevitable statistical comparison between Richardson's statistics and those of the previous season.

> Lockwood, whose career in first-class cricket had seemed to be over, came back to almost his finest form with the ball, but as a set-off against his restoration – no milder word will express the change that came over him – Richardson, and in a still more marked degree, Hayward fell a long way below the standard reached in the previous year. Richardson, it is true, wound up the season uncommonly well – bowling in irresistible fashion against Warwickshire at the Oval on the first days of September – but taking the whole summer through he was only the shadow of himself. In such a case as this figures can safely be trusted. In 1897 Richardson took, in county matches alone, 238 wickets, with an average of 14.55, whereas last season, playing in two matches less, he only took 126 wickets, with an average of something over 21. The difference of course was enormous. Having regard to the form in which he ended his season's labours, there is no reason to suppose that Richardson has permanently gone off. The more likely explanation is that he felt the effects of his hard work, during the winter, with Mr Stoddart's team in Australia. Fast bowlers cannot, with impunity, play cricket all the year round, and it would have been better for Surrey, as well as for his own reputation, if Richardson had not paid a second visit to the Colonies.[182]

---

180   of those taking ten wickets or more
181   *Cricket* 8 September 1898
182   *Wisden* 1899 p 60

1899

C.B.Fry was not alone in detecting a continuing decline in Richardson's effectiveness and looked back nostalgically to the halcyon days of only three seasons before:

> Tom Richardson had by 1899 begun to go off. In 1896 Tom had bowled magnificently in the Matches. He was a much bigger man than Lockwood. He was dark and black-haired – a cheerful brown-faced Italian-looking brigand with an ivory smile. Most genial, and an inexhaustible worker. He depended for his success upon sheer pace, perpetual accuracy, and an abrupt natural off-break.[183]

Richardson participated in the match at The Oval against Somerset which established a couple of records extant to this day. Coming in at 811 for 9, he was bowled by George Gill without further addition to the total, leaving Bobby Abel stranded on 357. He did, however, take four wickets in each innings as Surrey ran out winners by an innings and 379 runs.

It was again an Australian year, although there was never any chance that Richardson, now in decline, would be selected for England in the first home five-Test rubber, won 1-0 by the visitors. Notwithstanding their undefeated Test season, in a match recalled in an obituary appreciation of Richardson,[184] they came unstuck against Surrey at The Oval between the Fourth and Fifth Tests. The match swung Surrey's way with a second-innings 131 by Ernest Hayes, but Richardson played his part, ensuring Surrey's first innings reached three figures before becoming Hugh Trumble's eighth victim, but more significantly by taking out the middle order of Trumper, Gregory, Darling and Kelly on his way to four for 49 and a 104-run victory for the county.

Tom was granted a benefit in 1899, choosing the match against Lancashire which Surrey won by an innings and 121 runs and brought his total benefit fund to £1,000, including £50 from the Club. His contribution to the match was two not out and 33.3-16-75-4 and 20-9-49-2. The attendance was disappointing, as had been Richardson's season. He failed to reach a hundred first-class wickets, let alone the 250 plus of his glory days. Nevertheless, *Cricket* was suitably adulatory:

> As the weather at the beginning of this match was perfect, it was hoped that a very large crowd would appear at the Oval to do honour to the famous Surrey bowler who, although he has not been himself during the past two seasons, has done an immense amount of work for the last ten years, and has been the chief means of winning match after match for his side. If ever a man has deserved a magnificent benefit it is Richardson. It is sincerely to be hoped that many people who were not able to be at the ground will send in their subscriptions... At first sight it does not seem easy to see why the number of spectators was not larger, for Surrey men are not usually forgetful of their favourites, but the Lancashire team during recent matches has seemed to lose

---

183   *Life Worth Living* p 228
184   *Mitcham Advertiser* 12 July 1912

some of its attractiveness – it may be that the regretted absence of Briggs has taken some of the 'go' out of the team, and it is certain that its recent performances have not been such as to command great admiration, so that a well contested match was hardly to be looked for.[185]

A win against Hampshire took Surrey to the fringe of regaining the Championship title:

In the first innings, every bowler who went on distinguished himself, while Richardson ended up the innings in a remarkable manner.[186]

The 'remarkable manner' was 2.4-1-2-3 – all bowled. A heavily rain-affected draw against Warwickshire saw Richardson's team to the title which had eluded them for the previous three seasons. Apart from the truncated season of 1914 and the shared title of 1950, it was the last occasion until the run of seven consecutive Championships in the 1950s.

For Richardson, however, it had been a season of continuing decline, the weight gain first detected in Australia eighteen months before now becoming very apparent.

As Cecil Headlam pointed out:

When he did at last get a rest during the winter, he put on flesh alarmingly, and his great muscles turned to fat. He was summoned to explain himself before the Surrey Committee, when, aghast they beheld him, flabby, mountainous, and his pale face half gone, at the beginning of the next season. "Why, Tom, what on earth has happened to you?" "Well, gentlemen," replied Tom apologetically, "I suppose it is because I likes my creature comforts!"[187]

The anecdote is consistent with a comment by Ben Travers in *94 Declared*, who, born in 1886, might just have witnessed Richardson at his best and considered him England's greatest ever fast bowler. "However sceptical people may be about my estimate of Tom Richardson's bowling ability," he wrote, "one fact is universally acknowledged and unchallenged: he could and did drink a larger number of pints of beer on end than any known cricketer alive or dead."

Had Richardson been himself, there would have been a very different tale to tell, but the great fast bowler, who had put on a good deal of weight, was far less effective than in any year since he first played for Surrey, and his want of success made all the difference in the world to the eleven. It may be that a mistake was committed in not giving him more work to do in the early matches, but though as the summer advanced, he every now and then showed capital form, it cannot be said that he was ever the Richardson who had, in previous years, inspired batsmen with such a wholesome respect for his powers. In the seasons of 1893 to 1897 inclusive, the fact that they had to face

185   31 August 1899
186   *Cricket* 7 September 1899
187   Cecil Headlam *Behind the sticks in The Cricketer* 12 August 1922.

"O Tom, Tom! This will never do!"

Cartoon showing the expanding waistline which hastened the end of his career.

Richardson caused Surrey's opponents, no matter how good the wicket, to feel very apprehensive of what might happen but last summer the fast bowler had lost nearly all his terrors. Still under thirty years of age, he is quite young enough to recover his form, but to be again his old self he will certainly have to go into training, and get back to something like his former weight.[188]

1900

The season began with a win and a draw against new kids on the block, London County, at The Oval and Crystal Palace, Richardson's return in the latter being 27-2-122-4 including W.G.Grace and C.B.Fry. So there was still some life in the old dog, as demonstrated against Nottinghamshire in the traditional Whit Monday fixture. It was Shrewsbury's benefit match which Surrey won by four wickets, thanks in no small part to Richardson's second-innings 37.2-10-90-7, including the beneficiary, bowled for 22.

> Richardson bowled in something like his old form and it is evident that on a wicket which helps the bowlers a little, he is still a valuable man.[189]

W.T.Graburn, 'cricket instructor' at The Oval for most of the preceding decade, was able to put the season and Richardson's form in something of a historical context:

> As far as the present season is concerned, I see no reason to fear that we shall not do well. Richardson is still a very useful bowler to have on a side. One is apt to forget that a man cannot always take a couple of hundred wickets in a season, and just as one says that 'Ranji' is out of form if he doesn't make a hundred in nearly every innings, so one thinks about Richardson. But the chances are that he will take very nearly a hundred wickets this year, and a bowler who can do that must be a very good man indeed.[190]

He did – and followed it by exceeding a hundred in each of the following three seasons. So the decline was relative. By mid-season, apart from seven for 61 at Grace Road and seven for 90 at Trent Bridge, he had achieved little of distinction and lay 46th in the first-class averages with 59 wickets at 27.37. By contrast Rhodes headed the list with 138 at 11.71. However, fourteen wickets at Leyton (28.3-4-95-6 and 21.3-3-90-8 – six ball overs

---

188   *Wisden* 1900 p 2
189   *Cricket* 7 June 1900
190   *Cricket* 14 June 1900

now) saw an improvement in the statistics and a win for Surrey by an innings and 261 runs.

> ... the excellent bowling of Richardson who, helped a little by the wicket, was irresistible ...

The Essex innings was a great disappointment. Richardson was in his element and the only possible hope the batsmen could have had was to knock him off by determined cricket. Mr Owen and Mr McGahey made the attempt, and if fortune had been favourable it might have succeeded; they both played a great game. After their partnership, Richardson got the upper hand and there was no holding him. He took eight wickets for 90 runs and has hardly bowled better in his life.

. . . .

SCENE, Leyton. Richardson is smashing up the wickets in the Essex second innings.

First spectator (with much feeling) "Lord, 'ow I'd like to be the umpire at square leg !"
Second spectator: "Well, what if you was?"
First spectator: "What if I was? Why, you'd be surprised how soon I'd discover that Tom Richardson was chucking!"
Second spectator: "Struth! And to think that we can't do nothing except to set 'ere and cuss!"[191]

The Surrey team of 1900: Richardson is not yet 30 years of age,
but the weight gain is noticeable.
(Back row) T.Richardson, W.S.Lees, T.W.Hayward, E.G.Hayes, F.C.Holland,
F.Stedman, (seated) W.H.Lockwood, V.F.S.Crawford, D.L.A.Jephson (captain),
E.M.Dowson, W.Brockwell, (on ground) R.Abel, H.Wood.
[Messrs Gunn & Stuart, Richmond: Cricket 16 August 1900]

191   *Cricket*   19 July 1900

Not since the Trent Bridge Bank Holiday fixture in Richardson's first full season of 1893 had there been any serious suggestion of throwing. This was scarcely serious, rather the bucolic banter of partisan punters.

The revival continued against Sussex in a high scoring draw on what must have been a pretty flat track. His 18.5-2-76-5 and 26-2-116-6, the latter in an innings of 417 for 6, included C.B.Fry twice and Ranjitsinhji once, albeit for scores of 125, 229 and 103:

> The destroying angel was Richardson who, although he has not quite the same easiness of action which he possessed in his best days, has come to the front in an almost startling manner of late.[192]

192   *Cricket* 26 July 1900

Scorebook - Thames Ditton v Stoics 1900: Tom 7-51.
[Sutton History Centre and Thames Ditton Cricket Club]

Chapter Ten

The Twilight's Last Gleaming

1901

A brief paragraph in the *Daily Express* was drawn by Richardson to the attention of the Surrey committee. It followed a report that any prospect of a boat race between joint Yale/Harvard and Oxford/Cambridge Universities would need, because of the English universities' involvement in cricket, to be deferred until the autumn:

> We understand that Tom Richardson, whatever be his success with Surrey during the coming season, intends to make the present his last summer of first-class cricket. At times during last season, notably against Essex at Leyton and against Sussex at Brighton, the latter on a perfect wicket, Richardson bowled with all his old skill, and there is some ground for the opinion that if his heart 'were in it' and he trained, he might restore and retain those powers which made him the greatest and most untiring of all fast bowlers'.[193]

The committee decided to 'recommend him to take no proceedings'.[194]

Match-winning performances were now less frequent than they had been in earlier years, though one such was against the touring South Africans. His six wickets (for 50) in the first innings were six of the first seven in the batting order and his five for 75 in the second saw the county to a 59-run win. *Cricket* saw some synthesis between Richardson and Lohmann's protégé, the rising Jimmy Sinclair, both in the batsman-bowler duel and as contributors to their respective bowling attacks:

> Sinclair... made the best use of his height and strength and played Richardson early and well ...

> No one could make any stand against Mr Sinclair, who was as effective as Richardson had been.[195]

It was a fair comparison. Against Richardson's eleven for 125 in the match, Sinclair had thirteen for 153.

Richardson's best return that year was seven for 89 in the August Bank Holiday fixture at the The Oval and although at 23.25 runs per wicket, his average was higher than in the glory years, 159 wickets and ten five-wicket innings were testimony to an effectiveness that was still there, if less consistently so than in his earlier career. Only Wilfred Rhodes with 1,565.1 bowled more than his 1,293.4 overs.

---

193   28 March 1901
194   Surrey CCC minutes 17 April 1901
195   11 July 1901

A tailor's dummy with Tom Hayward.
[Roger Mann Collection]

In Lockwood's postponed benefit match against Yorkshire at The Oval, he again enjoyed himself briefly with the bat, scoring 28 – c Hirst b Rhodes – in a tenth-wicket partnership of 48 in half an hour with Jephson.

Aware that his career was coming to a close, he began to prepare for life after cricket:

> A letter was read from T.Richardson stating that he was taking over the Cricketers Inn Kingston in January but that it would in no way interfere with his commitment to the Surrey club. [196]

He began his post-cricket career with enthusiasm, refurbishing the premises –

> Tom Richardson, the Surrey County cricketer has now fairly established himself as "mine host" at the Cricketers' Inn, Kingston. He has made some much-needed improvements in the interior of the house.[197]

– and hosting the annual dinner of the Hodgsons' Kingston Brewery Cricket Club:

> Mr Tom Richardson catered for the company in a manner that gave the greatest satisfaction and he is to be congratulated upon his maiden effort at public catering.[198]

---

196   *Surrey CCC minutes* 18 December 1901.
197   *Surrey Comet* 5 February 1902
198   *Surrey Comet* 12 February 1902

The Cricketers at Kingston where Tom was licensee from January 1902.

He was keen to immerse himself in the local community, presumably with a view to increasing his turnover, joining Kingston Cricket Club, though there are no reports of his actually playing for them:

> Seven new members were elected including Tom Richardson, the Surrey County player. [199]

His involvement with charity matches continued:

> Tom Richardson has arranged two matches with the Mitcham Cricket Club against an eleven to be got together by him. It is hoped that the funds of the Kingston Victoria Hospital will be benefited by the visit of these players. [200]

He did not, however, sever his links with the Thames Ditton Club, attending their dinner at the end of the season.[201]

The pub is still there, a few hundred yards from Kingston town centre and overlooking the Fairfield Recreation Ground, its cricketing heritage surviving only in a well-used bat and pair of ancient pre-Velcro pads above the bar and an externally publicised facility to offer Sky Sports Live.

Furthermore, Tom was not alone in cashing in on his reputation as an established professional cricketer, to advertise commercial products, in this case, Recordine Embrocation, the Oilless Disinfectant.

Mr T.Richardson, Surrey County Cricket Club writes, Dec 3 1901

> I have used your Recordine with great benefit for sprains and bruises, and during the hot weather I have found a good rub down with your Embrocation before going into the field, and during the interval most refreshing. I also rub my feet with it, and find they keep me cool, and I find less fatigue. It is certainly the most pleasant Embrocation I have ever used, and I shall recommend it to all my friends. I may add that the other professionals are loud in its praises.[202]

Less expected perhaps was his apperance, along with Tom Hayward, as a fashion icon, advertising morning dress. A decade later he was singing the praises of Dr Williams' Pink Pills.

1902

The writing was perhaps on the wall for Tom when he was included in a squad of thirteen for what was now becoming the season's traditional opener against London County, but omitted from the final eleven. Although he usually opened the bowling there were occasions when he bowled first or second change. He did not take his fiftieth wicket until mid-July, reaching the nadir against Sussex at Hastings with 30-1-143-1 as Fry 's 159 and Ranjitsinhji's 234 not out saw Sussex to 705 for 8 declared, which remained the highest team total against Surrey until 1990.

---

199   *Surrey Comet* 15 March 1902
200   *Surrey Comet* 1 September 1902
201   *Surrey Comet* 25 October 1902
202   *Wisden* 1903 - back pages, not numbered.

However, matters improved after that and a season's best of seven for 53 against Somerset and seven for 63 against Middlesex accelerated the wickets total to 100 by the end of August and 106 in the season. He was still capable of bowling through an innings, indeed through both, and in the 291-run win against Lancashire at The Oval, he and Lockwood, but for two overs by Brockwell, would have bowled unchanged through the match.

> It was a bit of hard luck that Lockwood and Richardson should have by a mere accident missed last Saturday a distinction which does not fall to many bowlers in the course of a year of keeping up their ends unchanged during the two innings of a first-class game. Surrey's first two bowlers practically did this in the Lancashire match at the Oval at the end of the week. Lockwood, who had made a lot of runs in the first innings of Surrey, had rubbed one of his toes badly while batting, and had to consult a doctor with regard to its treatment between the innings, fearing that he might be prevented from continuing the game. As he had to have his foot attended to, a substitute had to take his place in the field for a few minutes. In his absence Brockwell had bowled two overs which he would not otherwise have done.[203]

It was about this time that Wilfred Rhodes took his 1,000th wicket in first-class cricket in his fifth season. Ashley-Cooper drew the inevitable comparison with Richardson's 1005 in his golden era of 1894/97. Rhodes' 1005 had cost 14,891 runs, Richardson's 14,154. Not a lot of difference, but Rhodes was – or was to become – an allrounder. Richardson never had any such pretensions.

In the match against Oxford University he reached 1,900 wickets and 3,000 runs, but he still had some pace, causing H.J.Wyld to retire hurt with a split finger.

At The Oval, the knives were out. He was no longer the effective match-winning, at times unplayable, bowler, of the 1890s. He was now disposable and the Committee sought to reduce his winter pay from £100 to £50. Though in terms of his value to the club this was a sensible and pragmatic decision, Richardson saw it as a breach of faith which, in terms of the 1895 agreement, it probably was. That 1895 agreement had referred only to an 'intention' to renew and there was now little prospect of its being continued at that level in subsequent winters. On a legal nicety the Club might have argued that an intention is not an obligation and in a case involving an unrepresented Richardson on one side and Lord Alverstone, President of the Club and Lord Chief Justice of England on the other, there would have been only one winner.

Eventually the Club fulfilled the moral obligation to restore the £100 but not without a bit of vigorous negotiating ping-pong:

> It was decided that Richardson should have notice that the arrangement with him on Aug 1 1895 and continued for a year on Sept 17 1901 would be discontinued. The question of any arrangement with

---

203   *Cricket* 21 August 1902

A Chat with Tom Richardson

The great Surrey cricketer recalls some note-worthy incidents in his career and pays a generous tribute to Dr. Williams' Pink Pills.

TOM RICHARDSON.

Whenever cricket is discussed the name of one man is almost sure to rise to the lips—that of genial Tom Richardson, the "demon" Surrey bowler and representative of his country in hard-fought test matches against Australia. To recount all his deeds on the green pitch would need a volume, but it will be remembered that Richardson's feat of capturing 1,005 wickets in four seasons has never been equalled by any other bowler.

During an interview at the Prince's Head, Richmond Green, of which he is the host, the question was put to the famous cricketer—"It would be interesting to know whether the stress of first-class cricket has any ill-effect upon a player?"

"That depends a great deal upon the man," was Mr. Richardson's reply; "but it is a fact that the nervous strain is almost sure to tell on the strength, sooner or later. When I retired from County Cricket my nervous system was impaired. I began to get upset over trivial matters. My appetite fell off, and my memory often failed me. But the most worrying trouble was Insomnia."

"Of course, this trouble made you feel heavy and languid?"

"Yes, it did. My nerves kept me restless by day as well as night, and almost any common-place event unnerved me. The result was that in time I began to get melancholy and depressed. I tired easily and got out of breath, I didn't feel inclined, in fact, to enthuse over anything. On various occasions I took medicines, but could trace no actual improvement."

"I suppose, like most men, you have had your share of Rheumatism?"

"Yes, I have, and that's a fact. I had disturbing twinges about the joints and my limbs felt stiff. Still, this was almost a blessing in disguise for an acquaintance happened to tell me that he had had a sharp attack of Rheumatism and had found relief in Dr. Williams' Pink Pills. So I took them for a time, and I must admit that I owe a good deal to this medicine."

"I had not taken Dr. Williams' Pink Pills for long when I began to feel brighter and more active. The Pills were a splendid tonic, and they sharpened my appetite so that I could sit down to a meal and enjoy it. Also, my nerves became steady again, and I was quite free from any signs of Rheumatism. I cannot speak too highly of the tonic virtues of Dr. Williams' Pink Pills."

Dr. Williams' Pink Pills are the finest tonic for all run-down conditions of the blood and nerves. They have cured repeatedly Rheumatism, Indigestion, Neuralgia, Nervous Disorders, and General Muscular Weakness. Obtainable of dealers or direct from Dr. Williams' Medicine Co., 46, Holborn Viaduct, London, post free, 2s. 9d. for one box, or 13s. 9d. for six boxes. Always ask for

Dr. Williams' Pink Pills

Advertisement for Dr Williams' Pink Pills.
[Wisden 1910]

Richardson was referred to the match committee.[204]

The Match Committee reported back recommending:

> ...that the engagement with Richardson entered into by the committee ...should be discontinued. It was resolved to recommend that Richardson be engaged for next summer and that he receive £50 for winter wages.[205]

The Committee had reckoned without Richardson's personal filing system and his knowledge of the workings of committees earned from his involvement with Thames Ditton Cricket Club. He had been street-wise enough to retain that crucial letter written to him seven years earlier.

The following letter was read from T.Richardson

> Dear Sir,
>
> In answer to yours of Nov 11 I wish to place my services for the season 1903 entirely in the hands of Surrey committee. At the same time I should like to draw their attention to their agreement with me of Aug 5 1895. That reads: The above agreement to be before the season of 1896 and to commence from the 1st of May 1896 with the intention of it being renewed as long as T.Richardson continues to play for the Surrey Club. I beg to remain

---

204   Surrey CCC minutes 4 September 1902
205   Surrey CCC minutes 6 October 1892

Your obt servant T.Richardson.

The consideration of the matter was deferred for consultation with the President.[206]

Subsequently –

> ...it was decided that the benefit given to Richardson in 1899 had ended the agreement made with Richardson on Aug 5 1895 and that any arrangement with Richardson be from year to year. The question of whether he should be considered a regular playing member of the eleven for 1903 was referred to the captain.[207]

Livingstone Walker, who decided that he should. However, between then and the start of the season

> It was decided that Richardson's winter wages for 1902-3 be one hundred pounds and that the Secretary inform Richardson that the matter must be reconsidered at the end of the season. [208]

The negotiations coincided with a difficult period in Richardson's private life. His third child Edith Norah had recently been born, the elder two, Tom and Kathleen being just five and two at the time. He was completing the first year of his tenancy of *The Cricketers Inn* in Kingston and it is possible that it was about this time he met his future 'housekeeper', Emily Birch, who was working in the refreshment room at the local railway station. His cricket career was clearly on the downward slope and, notwithstanding the bravado of his stance vis-à-vis the Committee, a speech he gave at New Malden makes clear the extent of his – possibly alcohol-induced – depression.

'PATHOS OF PROFESSIONALISM'

> Tom Richardson, the Surrey professional made a pathetic speech at a cricket club social gathering at New Malden.

> When a cricketer had reached the top of the ladder, he said, he found there was no enjoyment in the game, save when he was playing in charity matches, and thus helping others.

> He would never advise a young fellow to aspire to the position to which he had attained, for when one got to such a position one had such a long way to drop. That was the sad side of a professional cricketer's life.

> "I would that I had never aspired to the position I have held, because I am falling greatly," were the cricketer's final words.[209]

Richardson's weight was increasing, partly as a result of his alcohol intake – and it was not just beer. It was this season that his friend and admirer Herbert Strudwick began his long career with the county. Strudwick was a

---

206   Surrey CCC minutes 20 November 1902
207   Surrey CCC minutes 18 December 1902.
208   Surrey CCC minutes 19 March 1903
209   *Daily Express* 28 October 1902

teetotaller and at close of play one day picked up, by mistake, and drank a glass of ginger beer prepared for Tom Richardson. It had been laced with gin. Strudwick said it was the best ginger beer he had ever tasted.[210]

1903

This was Tom's last full season. He had 119 wickets, the tenth time in eleven full seasons that he had passed the hundred mark and on the other in 1899, had failed to do so only by two. His best was seven for 57 at Bramall Lane after five for 93 in the first innings. Never since the handful of matches played in his début season of 1892 had he failed to take seven wickets in an innings on more than one occasion *Cricket* variously reported:

> Only Findlay meeting with any pronounced success against Lockwood and Richardson ...

> Richardson being in great form ...

> Lockwood and Richardson soon became masters of the situation ...

> Richardson's bowling was quite a feature of the match.[211]

He played in the Gentlemen v Players match at The Oval, for the first time since 1897, but with only modest success – two wickets in each innings, an impressive 30.1-3-96-5 against Lancashire followed by 24.1-10-41-6 and 17.2-2-84-5 against Somerset:

> In both Somerset innings Richardson bowled admirably...

> On Tuesday afternoon, Richardson was even more successful with the ball than Braund had been on the previous day...[212]

He played against the touring Gentlemen of Philadelphia, his comments earning him a rare appearance in the *New York Times*. Swing bowling, spearheaded by George Hirst, was beginning to be a part of the cricket scene, and some saw the origins of this new 'swerve' bowling, as it was then called, in baseball pitching, adapted to the sister game by J.B.King. W.G.Grace apparently thought not too much of it, but Richardson was alive to its possibilities:

> The disregard of Dr Grace for this new style of bowling has not been shared by all his countrymen. Several bowlers since 1897 have endeavoured to imitate the American bowler who wrought such havoc at Brighton. Tom Richardson of Surrey is one of those who appreciates the importance of that 'curve in the air' and it is significant that many bowlers new to county cricket, men who have only gained their places on county teams within the last year or two, are credited with possessing the secret.[213]

As the season drew to a close, the whirligig of negotiations started up

210   McKinstry *Jack Hobbs* p 108
211   *Cricket* 2 July 1903
212   *Cricket* 23 July 1903
213   *New York Times* 16 August 1903.

again. This time there was no revolution:

> It was decided to give Richardson £50 instead of £100 as before.[214]

> Letter read from Richardson accepting the reduction to £50 in his winter wages but expressing the hope that the committee would again grant him £100 next year.[215]

1904

The end was now in sight. Tom played in only four Championship matches that season, then lost his place in the side and played a couple of matches for London County against Leicestershire and the touring South Africans.

When it came to contract negotiations, his position was not a strong one:

> It was decided to give Richardson fifty pounds to be a final payment if he would not accept a summer engagement only.[216]

He wouldn't.

The following letter from T.Richardson was read:

> Dear Sir

> I am obliged for your letter of the 18th October and must also express my thanks for the winter pay which the Committee has been good enough to grant me. I am sorry that the committee could not see their way to accept the terms I offered at our personal interview and sincerely regret having to sever my connection with the SCCC which I need hardly assure you will have my heartiest good wishes and command my keenest interest. The expression of the committee's good feeling towards me I esteem very much and I shall ever remember the kindly interest always extended to me by the members and yourself.

> Yours obediently

> T.Richardson.

Plaque commemorating opening of Mitcham Cricket Club's new pavilion in 1904.

214   Surrey CCC minutes 3 September 1903
215   Surrey CCC minutes 19 November 1903
216   Surrey CCC minutes 12 September 1904

Writing on the public reaction to Kipling's poem *The Islanders* ('flannelled fools at the wicket or the muddied oafs at the goals'), Albert Craig recorded that *Cricket* thought that the poet of Empire had made a mistake in judgment and that when Tom Richardson applied for the licence of the Cricketers Inn at Kingston the recorder asked him whether he had read Kipling's poem and the cricketer replied that he had and that he did not think much of it.

His career with Surrey was now over, but notwithstanding his likely failure to agree terms with the committee, there seems to have been no rancour or ill feeling, at least with his fellow professionals. In September he brought a Surrey XI to The Green to open Mitcham's new pavilion. The building is still in use.

For Surrey, however, it was a poor season, post-Richardson and pre-Hobbs. It was the end of an era. Not until the 1950s were they to emulate the Lohmann, Lockwood and Richardson-led successes of the 1880s and 90s:

> So far from showing the improvement that had been hoped for, the eleven met with even less success than in the previous summer, and had the worst season they have experienced for over twenty years.

> One could not without regret note the disappearance of Lockwood and Richardson – but the once incomparable fast bowlers had to go.[217]

Richardson, however, remained an icon, the benchmark against which others were measured. Writing on English cricket in the *Sydney Referee,* L.O.S.Poidevin said:

> They haven't got anybody who stands out as Richardson and Lockwood used to.[218]

Bath - 1905 to 1907

From 24 March 1905, Richardson had taken on the licence of the Wine Vaults on York Street in Bath, centrally situated and very close to the Abbey, the Roman Bath and the Pump Room, so clearly a busy district which must have been good for trade. Whether the move was just a wish to escape his broken marriage or whether he actually took the waters as a cure for the rheumatism – or maybe a bit of both – is unknown. He stayed there for two years, taking over from Thomas Baggs and in 1907 arranging to transfer the licence to his manager, Alfred Scott Tupling.[219]

The pub is still there, now renamed the *Ale House* in what has become a World Heritage site. It still has a turn-of-the-nineteenth/twentieth century appearance, the main bar and metalwork probably being very little changed from Richardson's day.

The sporting element remains, the wall behind the bar being festooned with the scarves of visiting rugby clubs – Leinster, Montpellier and sundry Welsh and Irish sides.

217   *Wisden* 1905 p 17
218   quoted in *Cricket* 22 December 1904
219   *Bath Chronicle* 28 March 1907

Instrumental in persuading Richardson to move west was the charismatic Sammy Woods, formerly of Australia and Surrey and now captain of Somerset, popular with the locals and prominent in sporting and civic circles. He had taken part in a function at the Palace Vaudeville Theatre to raise funds for the Bath Association Cricket Club which had a deficit on its general account and a sizeable debt on its new pavilion. The 'ever popular Somerset skipper' sang a 'droll ditty', 'Always keep a night-light by your bed'.[220]

The Bath Cricket Week, which in 1905 involved Championship fixtures for Somerset against Gloucestershire and Hampshire, took place in early June on the Recreation Ground. There is no evidence that Richardson was in any way involved, but there was a prescient passage in the local newspaper, anticipating a 'road' for the July fixture against the captain's compatriots:

> The wicket for the Australian game next month is a little to the right of those that will be used during the Week and should play splendidly. It has been given a top dressing of clay. It is to be hoped that the Bath pitches this time will be given the test of three full days play, which they have never been called upon to stand.[221]

A week later Richardson put on the whites again to play for Bath and District against the Rest of the County in a charity match to raise funds for the Royal United Hospital. Opposing him in the visiting team was Sammy Woods who took half a dozen wickets, including that of Richardson for a duck. The declining former fast bowler reciprocated with two, but one was that of his friend and former colleague:

> ...'Sammy' being bowled after a capital innings by Tom Richardson when the fast bowler got 'Sammy's' wicket the applause was loud and it was a remarkable incident that the great 'Tom' should have upset the redoubtable Somerset skipper.[222]

Perhaps it was this occasion that caused Woods to persuade Richardson to turn out for Somerset in the mid-July fixture against the Australians. He played, but with no success, conceding 65 runs at five an over without taking a wicket. Those who had played against him a decade earlier must have been astonished at the decline and those touring England for the first time could only speculate on what a magnificent bowler Richardson must have been in his prime.

With Victor Trumper and Warwick Armstrong opening the batting, it was a complete mismatch as Armstrong recorded a career-best 303 not out and Monty Noble at No.4 had a century, enabling the tourists to declare at 609 for four. Somerset followed on and managed to avoid an innings defeat, but for Richardson, it was a forlorn end to a distinguished career. In a recent article in *The Guardian* David Foot compared the pathos with that of Wally Hammond's last appearance on the first-class scene in 1951:

> Curly's appearance was a disaster, mocking as it did the fast bowler's

---

220   *Bath Chronicle* 20 April 1905
221   *Bath Chronicle* 1 June 1905
222   *Bath Chronicle* 15 June 1905

The Ale House (formerly the Wine Vaults) where Tom was licensee during his two year sojourn in the West Country.

bountiful career and all those wickets he earned by sweat, natural prowess and instinctive, pacy technique. He was introduced as second change, something of a demotion for the former England opening bowler, and took no wickets in 13 overs of medium-paced dross.

Tom must have been tempted to have one final go at the Australians, but, as Foot continues, 'fallibility and bad judgement remain an absorbing feature of the human condition.'[223]

The local press expressed similar sentiments at the time:

> Nobody imagined that Somerset could get the better of a side which it takes the pick of England to beat, but the County did the next best thing and avoided defeat. The Somerset bowling was known to be weak, but its lack of sting was never more forcibly demonstrated.

> The inclusion of Tom Richardson was a surprise to Bathensians. They do not see him bowling on the North Parade ground in club matches now, and presumably it was for this department of the game he made one of the Somerset eleven against Australia. It is pretty evident that the bowler whose presence was once a terror to many when in his prime must be content to rest satisfied with the abundant honours and glory he has already won in the cricket field. Younger talent should be encouraged.[224]

There is an implication that he had turned out for Bath Cricket Club and indeed in the Club's 150th Anniversary publication, he is listed among international cricketers who have appeared on the ground,[225] but he clearly did so no more.

It was a poor season for Somerset:

> The redoubtable S.M.J. who as captain has had to put up with difficulties and limitations which would worry a less cheery soul .....[226]

Woods survived one more season as captain: Richardson played no more first-class cricket. The following season he appeared for L.C.Braund's XI in a two-day match against a Scotland XI in Glasgow, but his playing career was essentially over.

Richmond – 1907 to 1912

There is a later reference to his playing for Marriott's XI in a cricket week match at Ashford (Middlesex) Cricket Club about 1908 'although he had retired from serious cricket then'.[227] He was now able to concentrate on his new rôle, not unfamiliar to retired cricketers, as mine host of his third pub, in this case the *Prince's Head* on Richmond Green.

The pub's origins can be traced to the eighteenth century when it was

223   David Foot *The Guardian* 24 June 2009
224   *Bath Chronicle* 20 July 1905
225   p 31
226   *Bath Chronicle* 31 August 1905
227   Ashford C C website

Richardson's last home – the Prince's Head on Richmond Green.

known as the *Duke's Head* after the second Duke of Ormonde (1665-1745) whose claim to fame rests on his victory at Vigo Bay in 1702 in the War of the Spanish Succession and to notoriety on his impeachment for treason. As a consequence of the latter the establishment was re-engineered as the *Prince's Head*.

A local journalist, Royman Browne, was to suggest later that the pub be renamed *The Fast Bowler* in honour of its most famous licensee. The idea was supported by the landlord at the time, Cyril Muller, the owning brewery Fuller, Smith and Turner – and by John Arlott who wrote:

> What a great idea to call the Prince's Head the 'Fast Bowler' in honour of Tom Richardson. There are many pub princes and dukes of all sorts, but this would be a unique and worthwhile naming because, after all, Tom Richardson was the classic fast bowler.[228]

The idea was, however, not pursued.

By this time, Richardson's marriage had broken down, but the children continued to live with him at the *Prince's Head* along with a 'housekeeper', a couple of servants described as a barmaid and a domestic, and a lodger.

His wife, Edith, was working as a nanny in Putney. She appears on the 1911 Census as a 'maternity nurse' to Mr Alfred Patterson, a postman, and his wife who have two daughters aged three and one month. She is

---

228   *Richmond and Twickenham Times* 16 August 1958

described in the transcript as Mr Patterson's 'niece' , but as he is aged only 24 and was born in Carlisle, Mrs Patterson 26 and born in Cornwall, the relationship appears an unlikely one and a more likely explanation is that the word is a mistranscription of 'nurse'. It is unlikely that she and Tom would have been divorced. There were well under a thousand divorces per annum in the whole country, compared with over one hundred thousand now, it was many years before the ethos of 'no fault' and Tom may have been a Roman Catholic. Within a few years his funeral cortège would leave from Richmond's Roman Catholic church, though the marriage had been in Beddington Parish Church.

The change in Tom's personal circumstances caused him to draw up a will. Richardson's marriage to Edith came to an end some time between the birth of his youngest child, Edith Norah, in the summer of 1902, and his

Richardson's handwriting on his 1911 Census entry for the Prince's Head, Richmond Green showing his family, 'housekeeper' and domestic staff.

return from Bath to Richmond in 1907. In his last will and testament drawn up on 6 July the following year, he bequeathed his piano, music stool and accessories to Kathleen May, watch and chain, personal jewellery, cricket balls and mementoes to Tom William Gresham as heirlooms,[229] his silver coffee service to Edith Norah 'and all my furniture linen and household effects to Emily Birch in order that she may provide my infant children with a home'. She was also bequeathed one-quarter of the residual estate (the other three-quarters to be held in equal shares for the children until they reached their majority) and appointed guardian of the children. His estranged wife, Edith, features nowhere in the document. Emily Birch who was three years younger than Tom, had in her teens been in service

---

229   They did not all remain in the family. David Frith mentions in his autobiography that he bought from Tom's son the mounted cricket balls from the 10-45 against Essex in 1894 and 8-94 at Sydney in 1897/98 (*Caught England, Bowled Australia* p 257)

in Aylesbury before becoming manageress of the refreshment room at Kingston upon Thames railway station, then Tom's 'housekeeper'.[230]

She was very evidently more than that. Housekeepers are not as a general rule major beneficiaries or appointed to be guardians of the testator's children. Newspapers at the time were not intrusive into sportsmen's private lives and no evidence has been found as to whether Emily was the cause or the result of Tom's break with Edith. Marital break-ups, mistresses and repartnering are now the bread and butter of tabloid journalism, but there was no mobile phone hacking in those days.

One of Tom's executors was William Strutt-Cavell, a 'sporting reporter', to whom Albert Craig was to dedicate a poem and who, four years later was to make most of Richardson's funeral arrangements. In the grant of probate, he is described in Gilbert and Sullivan terms as '(in the will called 'Will')'. The other executor was Percival Coles who played a little first-class cricket with Sussex and Oxford University and played for three years in the Oxford University rugby XV, the last of them as captain. He was a founder member of the Barbarians and the first paid Secretary of the Rugby Football Union.[231] It is not clear how or where he might have crossed paths with Richardson. It was probably in the *Prince's Head*. It is not a million miles from Twickenham. Both executors are described as 'friends'.

In July 1909, with the death of Albert Craig, Surrey lost one of its keenest supporters and admirers. His funeral on 12 July was attended by club officials and by eleven past and present players, including Tom Richardson. Ironically it was three years almost to the day before Tom's own funeral.

Still a name in cricketing circles, although no longer active, Tom appeared once again in *Wisden* in 1910, outside the record pages, extolling the virtues of Dr Williams' Pink Pills.

---

230   Censuses of Population 1891, 1901 and 1911
231   Wikipedia

THIS IS THE LAST WILL AND TESTAMENT OF THOMAS RICHARDSON

of me THOMAS RICHARDSON of The Princes Head Richmond Green in the County of Surrey Licensed Victualler I appoint my friends Will Strutt-Cavell and Percival Coles (hereinafter called "my trustees") to be the EXECUTORS and trustees of this my Will I give my piano music stool and accessories to my daughter Kathleen May I give my watch and chain my personal jewellery the cricket balls presented to me during my cricket career and all my cricket mementoes to my son Tom William Gresham as heirlooms I give to my daughter Edith Norah my silver coffee service I give all my furniture linen and household effects to Philip Birch in order that she may provide my infant children with a home And as to all the rest residue and remainder of my property whatsoever and wheresoever both real and personal I give devise and bequeath the same unto my trustees Upon trust to sell call in and convert into money the same and to divide the proceeds of such sale and conversion and my ready money into four equal parts And as to one of such equal parts to pay the same to the said Emily Birch absolutely And as to the remaining three equal fourth parts or shares in trust to invest the same in some or one of the modes of investment authorised by law for the benefit of my said children namely Kathleen May Tom William Gresham and Edith Norah in equal shares upon their respectively attaining the age of twenty one years And I declare that my trustees may at their discretion during the respective minorities of any of my said children apply any part or parts not exceeding in the whole one moiety of the capital of the share to which each or any of such children shall be entitled under this my Will in or towards the advancement in life or otherwise for the benefit of such child And I appoint the said Emily Birch to be the guardian of my infant children IN WITNESS whereof I have hereunto set my hand this sixth day of July one thousand nine hundred and eight - TOM RICHARDSON - Signed by the testator in our presence and by us in his - PHILOT HUZARD Solr 15 Abchurch Lane London E C - O L RICHARDSON Articled with the above

OO the 24th day of August 1912 Probate of this Will was granted to William Strutt-Cavell one of the Executors.

WILL

DEATH ON OR AFTER 1st JANUARY, 1898.

BE IT KNOWN that *Thomas Richardson*
of The Princes Head Richmond
Green in the County of Surrey

died on the 2ⁿᵈ day of *July* 19/2
at *Saint Je.... Paris in France*

AND BE IT FURTHER KNOWN that at the date hereunder written the last Will and Testament

of the said deceased was proved and registered in the Principal Probate Registry of his Majesty's High Court of Justice, and that administration of all the estate which by law devolves to and vests in the personal representative of the said deceased was granted by the aforesaid Court to *William (: the will called will) Strutt-Cavell of 14 Napoleon Road Twickenham in the County of Middlesex Sporting reporter being the Executor*

named in the said *will power reserved to the other executor*

Dated the 24ᵗʰ day of *August* 19 /2

Gross value of Estate £627 : 17 : 0
Net value of Personal Estate £ /55 : / : /

IA.

Tom Richardson's last will and testament and grant of probate.

Chapter Eleven
Technique and Personality

Tom Richardson's bowling technique was of the simplest. His 6ft 1½ in, 12st 7lb frame[232] simply accelerated to the crease, leapt in the air and bowled with a high sideways on action, his right arm sweeping across his body to finish across his left thigh and his fingers running across whatever might remain of the seam, thereby imparting what his contemporaries called 'break' and what we would call 'cut'. Whatever it was called, it was prodigious and it was consistent.

Nothing else, no variation of pace or angle, no Lohmann-style 'hanging ball', negligible inconsistency, deliberate or otherwise, in line and length. His great attribute was that he could go on and on, over after over, hour after hour, match after match and season after season, his great career reaching a plateau between 1893 and 1897. Unlike many bowlers who have revelled in damp uncovered pitches, Richardson was, because of his pace, unable to get a foothold in damp conditions and, although there are instances of success on wet pitches, it was not in his temperament to change his pace or style and consequently most of his great performances were on hard, fast pitches in what would, but for Richardson, have been unquestionably batsman-friendly conditions.

No fast bowler can reasonably be expected to remain at his fastest for more than four or five years. Fred Trueman and Allan Donald were rare exceptions but for most, like Frank Tyson, it was two or three. Others like Ray Lindwall and Dennis Lillee, after injury in the case of the latter, adjusted their style to compensate for declining speed by concentrating more on variations of pace, swing and cut. Richardson was not like that. His decline was almost as rapid as his rise and with rare exceptions he was never the same bowler again after that debilitating 1897/98 tour of Australia:

> Richardson made a noble sight, a giant with black curly hair and a moustache; he ran to bowl in swinging strides and just before his arm wheeled over he leapt upwards: it was like a wave going to a crest then breaking.[233]

or, Cardus again:

> This man Richardson was the greatest cricketer that ever took to fast bowling. Lockwood had nicer technical shades than Richardson – a guile which was alien to the honest heart of Richardson. But Lockwood had not a great spirit. He was a bowler at the mercy of a mood; an artist

---

232   *Lillywhite's* 1897 p 293
233   Cardus *Autobiography* p 36

with an artist's capriciousness. Richardson bowled from a natural impulse to bowl, and whether he bowled well or ill that impulse was always strong. His action moved one like music because it was so rhythmical. He ran to the wicket a long distance, and at the bowling crease his terminating leap made you catch breath. His break-back most cricketers of his day counted among the seven wonders of the game. He could pitch a ball outside the wicket on the hardest turf and hit the leg stump. The break was, of course, an action break; at the moment of release his fingers swept across the ball and the body was flung towards the left. And his length was as true as Attewell's own.

Cardus then went on to say,

> His bowling was wonderful because into it went the very life-force of the man – the triumphant energy that made him in his hey-day seem one of Nature's announcements of the joy of life. It was sad to see Richardson grow old, to see the fires in him burn low.[234]

Such is the poetic version of Richardson's action. Bettesworth also appreciated the aesthetics of the action:

> It is a splendid sight to see Richardson bowling, when in form. Every action of his, the run, the swing of the arm, denoted power, and one derived the same satisfaction watching him, as one derives from watching an express engine in full career, with the vast difference that the bowler is not a machine.[235]

Others are more mundane and technically analytical. Given Cardus's admiration of Richardson, it is perhaps scarcely surprising that arguably the game's greatest author should choose arguably the game's greatest fast bowler as one of his six Cricketers of the Wisden Century in 1963. Although not untypically cavalier in his approach to facts – some of the statistics given lack a little in accuracy and Cardus mentions five-ball overs in Australia in 1897/98 when in fact there were six – he remains confident of his judgment of Richardson's place in the fast-bowling firmament:

> I choose Richardson as one of my Six, not on the supposition that he was the greatest fast bowler of the century, though certainly he was in the running. I take him as the fully realised personification of the fast bowler as every schoolboy dreams and hopes he might one day be himself.[236]

Compared with present-day bowlers, Richardson had the advantage of bowling on uncovered pitches, but the disadvantage of bowling most of his overs on Sam Apted's immaculate surfaces and of pre-dating the new ball regulations, so he was obliged to bowl whole innings with the same ball, almost seamless when he started and entirely so by the time he had finished, having on numerous occasions bowled through a complete innings. His flowing action, vigorous body movement and final sweep of the arm ensured a sharp break-back achieved independently of the

---

234   *A Cricketer's Book* pp 49-50
235   *Chats on the Cricket Field* pp 357-358
236   *Wisden* 1963 p 99

condition of the ball. A further disadvantage compared with his modern counterparts is that the LBW law was more favourable to batsmen before it was changed in 1935. In Richardson's day the ball had to pitch between wicket and wicket for the bowler to have a chance. So in theory the batsman could safely pad up to anything pitched outside the off stump. In practice, given the flimsy nature of protective equipment, it might have been masochistic to do so against some one of Richardson's pace, but it is at least arguable that, had the current lbw law been in operation then he might have had even more than his 2,104 first-class wickets.

If anything he was perhaps too consistent. He hardly ever bowled a loose ball, but Ranjitsinhji expressed a preference for Richardson's bowling over Lockwood's on the grounds that it was more predictable and less variable:

> On a good wicket Tom's speed and breakback needed watching, but I knew what was coming. With Lockwood I had to keep awake for his slower ball.[237]

He was able to speak with authority, having in his salad days at Cambridge University hired both Richardson and Lockwood to bowl to him to help him acclimatise to English bowlers and conditions.[238]

George Lohmann, Richardson's opening partner in the demolition of Australia at Lord's in 1896, the only occasion on which they bowled together for England, had no doubt about his colleague's place in the world bowling league. He had seen them all, English, Australian and South African and, even with an allowance for Surrey bias, unhesitatingly places his friend right at the top:

> In my opinion he is the best bowler in the world on a good wicket... If he could only get a footing on sticky wickets his average would be about half what it is now; as it is, about a third of the runs that are made off him are due more to accident than intention. He is one of the best triers I have ever seen and one of the best tempered.[239]

With the advantage of hindsight, Long Leg in his *Sporting Life* obituary of Richardson sixteen years later, saw no reason to modify that judgment:

> Many fine judges of cricket – among them the Hon R.H.Lyttelton – did not hesitate to describe Richardson as the finest fast bowler the world had ever seen. He had not S.M.J.Woods's power of pace changes, or quite so much speed as Ernest Jones, nor did he come so quickly off the pitch as Lockwood or Mold: but he had far more accuracy than the Australian, as much pure speed as any of the others, and he was easily their master in point of consistency. He was totally unlike the majority of fast bowlers who have succeeded him; bowlers who bang the ball down short on the off side and trust to catches in the slips and at the wicket to bring them success. No; Richardson aimed at the stumps and owed comparatively little to his fieldsmen... I think it is right to say that a large proportion of the runs scored from him were

237   *Wisden* 1963 p 101
238   Dobbs *Edwardians at Play* p 132
239   Bettesworth *Chats on the Cricket Field; George Lohmann* 30 July 1896.

the result of lucky snicks through the slips or to leg about which the batsman knew nothing, than was the case with any other bowler of his generation ... His pronounced off-break coupled with his great pace made him particularly difficult to score from in front of the wicket. There were times when it seemed scarcely necessary for him to have any fieldsman, beyond the wicket-keeper.

He had such splendid legs and thighs and such beautifully developed muscles in the back. To quote another apt description of C.B.Fry's: "Most of his action comes from the small of his back which must have double action, Damascus steel fittings."

He was essentially a natural bowler. He took a very long run – fully twenty yards... Every foot of it had purpose... It was a straight forward run made up of long strides, rhythmical, elastic, and the whole impetus of it was put into the high, swinging rotary action. His delivery had no suspicion of laboriousness. His body swung and the way his hand cut across the ball gave him what is called 'action-break' which is totally different from finger-spin break, so different that Richardson could command his three to six inches of sudden off-break on a pitch so true that the finger-spinners were coming along quite plain. There were those who called him purely a mechanical bowler. Perhaps he was. But a man who could average his 250 wickets a season in first-class matches for four years had no need to strive after generalship. He had something better than that. He had the devastating power of artillery.[240]

Unlike his Australian contemporary Ernest Jones, Richardson was not a 'nasty' bowler. In his biography of W.G.Grace, Simon Rae relates an instance of the man's gentle nature. It was the return match against Gloucestershire in 1895:

Surrey had their revenge for the defeat at The Oval when they came to Clifton towards the end of August. Richardson, who was on fine form, bowled Grace for a duck and the whole team was out for 53. At a reception for the players of both teams that evening the host took the Surrey fast bowler aside and congratulated him on his performance, but insisted that 'The Old Man must not get a pair'. The following morning Richardson, 'the most good-natured of men', obliged with an easy one, but Grace was almost immediately dismissed by Hayward for 3.[241]

Known as 'Long Tom' because of his height or 'Honest Tom' because of his 'honest toil', the 'bouncer' – in its infancy at the time and not to become a regular part of the game before the 'bodyline' series – was not part of his fast bowling armoury and when the unreliable nature of the pitch or the batsmen's own incompetence caused him to be hit, Richardson was generally the first to show concern.

---

240   *Sporting Life* 5 July 1912
241   *W G Grace: A Life* p 415: 'the most good-natured of men' is from the *Memorial Biography.*

Richardson at the Oval nets. Maurice Read is the next to bowl.
[Roger Mann Collection]

The already famous ball by which Jones creates terror in batsmen, even if he does not get their wicket by it, generally pitches rather under half way than over. It comes so quickly off the pitch that a batsman seems only to have just time to get his nose out of the way and is as likely as not to touch it with his bat without intending to do so. It remains to be seen whether Richardson can develop a similar ball.[242]

Three seasons later he had not and clearly had no intention of so doing:

> even Richardson, when he was in all his glory, had not the infinite variety of Jones – possibly because he did not care to make use of the very short-pitched ball, which is so terrifying in the hands of the expert.[243]

This is clearly the bumper or bouncer, now referred to in Law 42 as 'dangerous and unfair bowling' and preceding by almost forty years its refinement into leg-theory and bodyline and by about twice that the now ubiquitous helmet. There is no doubt that Richardson could have developed a similar ball. There is equally no doubt that it was totally alien to his nature to have done so. 'Infinite variety' was not part of his armoury.

A century and more later, Simon Wilde is able to take a longer-lens view and place Richardson in his historical context as a successor to Spofforth, the *primus inter pares* of his own generation, unique in his way and a hero and rôle model for succeeding generations:

> By the time the lessons of Spofforth were fully absorbed, fast bowling had been transformed. Technically and physically, Tom Richardson formed the perfect conclusion to the overarm revolution: tall and superbly built and operating off a long run, he delivered the ball with a high right arm and smooth rotation of the body, imparting it with genuine speed and a vicious break from the off. Always aiming to bowl

---

242 *Cricket* 14 May 1896
243 *Cricket* 1 June 1899

at the stumps... Richardson never moderated his pace. His method was so fluid that he barely needed to – he could bowl unchanged for hours without compromising his pace, length or off-break – and by dint of his extraordinary character, did not want to: he loved bowling and was a glutton for hard work.[244]

Whether he was a chucker is open to debate and in the absence of film or video evidence is impossible to settle. There was certainly controversy in that early Bank Holiday match at Trent Bridge. Rev R.S.Holmes was convinced that his action was legitimate and the suspicion arose from an over-extended wrist.

On the other hand, in nominating Richardson as one of its Five Cricketers of the Year, *Wisden* took the view that the action had been highly suspect, but he had taken steps to correct it.

Whatever comparisons are made with contemporaries and others, whatever technical analysis may be applied to his action and tactics, outstanding and separating him from the rest, as it did at Old Trafford in 1896, is his remarkable and probably unparalleled stamina:

> even more remarkable than his speed and his sharp off-break was his enduring energy, his cheerful love of hard tasks and hard work, his refusal to abdicate before fatigue. Other bowlers have had more subtleties, and many have lasted for longer, but none has shown the consistency and persistency and undergone greater toil than did Richardson between the years 1893 and 1898. In those days he could bowl for hours without losing pace or sting, and an off-day seemed unknown to him...

> Hour after hour, day after day, week after week, he kept up an end for Surrey in some of the hottest weather known in this country – and remember he was a bowler who took a tremendous lot out of himself, although he was physically an exceedingly strong man.[245]

His enthusiasm for bowling was unquestionable. Until 1900, the five-ball over was the norm in England. When asked for an opinion as to whether it should be increased to six, he is reputed to have replied: 'Give me ten.'[246]

His remarkable powers of stamina perhaps owed something to the fact that he made little attempt to bat or field, though *Lillywhite*'s annual bland comments did acknowledge some ability in the first area and some improvement in the second.

The first appearance in 1894 records:

> One of the very best fast bowlers of the day, keeps a good length and comes back at times a good lot. Can bat well. Wants to be a little smarter in the field.

244   *The World's Best Batsmen and Bowlers* pp 77-80
245   *Sporting Life* 5 July 1912
246   John Woodcock *One Hundred Greatest Cricketers* 46

*Balls with which Richardson took 10-45 against Essex in 1894 and 8-94
in his last Test match v Australia at the SCG in 1898.*
*Along with the cap they were bought by David Frith from Richardson's son,
Tom, to whom his father bequeathed as heirlooms his watch and chain and
personal jewellery and the cricket balls presented during his career and all his
cricket mementoes. The cap was, according to Tom junior, Richardson's England
cap. They are now numbered chronologically, beginning with Tom Armitage
at 1. The most recent in2012 is Samit Patel. Tom's would have been
88, Brockwell's 87. However it was not until after the establishment of the
Board of Control in 1899 that caps were physically awarded: so it appears to be
an anachronism, either awarded retrospectively and sentimentally…
or it belonged to someone else.*
[David Frith Collection]

Apart from a correction to the address, the entry remains the same for the
following year, but by 1896, the angle has changed slightly:

> … took 237 wickets for Surrey last season and 290 in all first-class
> matches: can bat well and is a good field.[247]

The *Sporting Life* was more honest and more critical:

> Perhaps Richardson should be described as a fast bowler rather than a
> thorough cricketer – although no one ever put his heart and soul into a
> game to a greater extent, but while he stopped and caught most things
> that came to him at mid-off where he generally fielded he was not a
> good field; and although he more than once made a useful score, his
> batting was unorthodox in the extreme. Yet he had a good eye, and was
> always a delight to the Oval crowd with his hitting that carried the ball
> very high – when he happened to hit it.[248]

Herbert Strudwick attributes to Richardson the unusual characteristic of
being able to recollect statistical detail of matches in which he has played

---

247   *Lillywhite's* 1894 p 244, 1895 p 233, 1896 p 288.
248   5 July 1912

and of knowing the number of runs scored against each bowler in matches in which he was playing:

> Tom Richardson had a wonderful memory. After many years, if a match in which he had played was referred to, he would recall the actual score, including individual batsman [sic] and bowling analysis. Also, coming off the field after an innings of perhaps 300, he could tell each bowler the number of runs scored against him.[249]

It is a skill not given to many – though most bowlers will have an approximate idea of what they have conceded – and one appreciated by Strudwick, Surrey scorer for thirty years. Some of his successors have difficulty remembering what happened in the previous evening's Twenty20.

Off the field 'Honest Tom' was an affable man with a genial personality:

> Tom Richardson was more than a great fast bowler – he was a great-hearted man and picturesque personality. He did something finer than the winning of many matches for his county and his country – he won the affection of all who came to know him.[250]

Nicknamed 'Curly' from his early days at Mitcham, he never seemed to resent it, even when it was used by the younger generation:

> From the start he was a favourite with all the boys – we used to call him Curly! We would go up to him and say "Hullo Curly!" Tom would always smile and cry "Hullo kiddies!"[251]

Despite the fearsome figure he presented to opposing batsmen:

> in private life he was of an engagingly gentle nature – indeed, a very loveable man.[252]

This description which is confirmed elsewhere is in sharp contrast to his New Malden comments and to what Richardson in his advertisement for Dr Williams' Pink Pills[253] says about depression and insomnia. If that were believable, there might be some credibility in the suicide theory that was to follow his death. However, it was said for commercial purposes, newspapers, magazines and books at the time being full of scarcely believable quack remedies guaranteed to cure anything from stress to syphilis. The Advertising Standards Authority was not around then.

---

249   *Mitcham Cricket Club Yearbook* 1937: *Snapshots from "Struddy's" recollections*
250   'Long Leg' in *Sporting Life* 5 July 1912
251   Strudwick *25 Years Behind the Stumps* p 29
252   *Sporting Life* 5 July 1912
253   Dr Williams' Pink Pills for Pale People were an iron-based tonic for the blood and nerves used in the treatment of anaemia, clinical depression, poor appetite and loss of energy. They were widely advertised with an abundance of anecdotal evidence. (In his endorsement of them in the 1910 edition of *Wisden*, Richardson says they helped cure his insomnia, depression and rheumatism.) The patent for the pills was bought in 1890 by Senator George T Fulford (1852-1905), an American politician, and there were subsequent claims for the successful treatment of neuralgia, spring chills, consumption and even paralysis.

Chapter Twelve
Bout-du-Monde

On 13 July 1912 the Gentlemen v Players match at The Oval was drifting to a draw. Between 3.50 and 4.10 play was suspended and the flags lowered to half-mast. At Giggs Hill Green, too, Thames Ditton's club match was adjourned for half an hour as his former friends and colleagues paid their respects, the time deliberately chosen to coincide with that when Tom Richardson's coffin would reach Richmond cemetery, having left the Catholic church at the Vineyard an hour before.

Eleven days earlier, his body had been discovered in open country in the foothills of the French Alps. It was a tragic and premature death. For some time it was considered to be suicide. There is, however, no evidence for this beyond phrases such as 'tragic end'[254] and 'in such tragic circumstances'.[255] It seems too much has been read between the lines; any death at a premature age may be regarded as 'tragic', the more so when it is that of a fine professional athlete, gone to seed and overweight at the age of 41. Research undertaken by the late Ralph Barker and described in part of his book[256] and an article[257] seems to have exploded that myth.

Richardson was staying at the time at Aix-les-Bains, famous for its sulphur baths attracting in the late nineteenth and early twentieth centuries genuine patients, hypochondriacs and 'a rabble of nobilities, big and little, here all the time, and often a king or two, but as these behave quite nicely and keep themselves to themselves, they are little or no annoyance'.[258] Queen Victoria was an earlier visitor under the pseudonym of 'Countess of Balmoral'.[259] In addition, the town stood second in France only to Monte Carlo in the number of visitors there for the attractions of the casino.

It epitomised the *belle époque* of the late nineteenth and early twentieth centuries, the nearest English equivalents then and now would be Cheltenham and Harrogate.

Some hotels had their own spas and baths; patients staying elsewhere who were incapable of walking or unwilling to do so were transported in a sort of sedan chair to the public establishments.

You see nothing of the patient in this diving-bell as the bearers tramp

---

254   *Daily Mail* 4 July 1912, *Mitcham Advertiser* 12 July 1912, *Wisden* 1913 p 195
255   *Mitcham Advertiser* 19 July 1912
256   *Ten Great Bowlers* pp 124-126
257   *Cricketer* 1966 [pp30-31]
258   *Daily Tribune, Chicago* 8 November 1891: Mark Twain *Travel Letters*
259   Aix-les-Bains Tourist Guide website

along, except a glimpse of his ankles bound together and swathed around with blankets or towels to that generous degree that the result suggests a sore piano leg. By attention and practice the pallbearers have got so that they can keep out of step all the time – and they do it. As a consequence their veiled chum goes rocking, tilting, swaying along like a bell-buoy in a ground swell. It makes the oldest sailor sea-sick to look at that spectacle.[260]

Mark Twain had been at Aix-les-Bains in 1891 seeking a cure for rheumatism in his right arm and recorded his impressions of the place for a Chicago newspaper. What Richardson was doing there is less transparent, nor is there any evidence as to whether this was his first visit or one of a series. The presence of nurses mentioned in the *Daily Mail* report suggests that it was for medical reasons. Barker, basing his evidence on an interview with Tom Richardson junior, states that Tom suffered from rheumatism.[261] If that is so – and Ranjitsinhji's comments on the 1897/98 tour of Australia confirm it – it would explain the reason for one or more visits to a spa town in France, but there may have been another reason and there are clues in the location of his hotel – immediately opposite the casino and the baccarat tables for which it was renowned – as well as the amount of money later found on his body.

He was accompanied by a Mr and Mrs Owers. The *Sporting Life* later mentions 'A and D.Owers'[262] as his hosts at Chambéry, probably the same people and a 'Mr J.Owers'[263] had seen to all the arrangements in France.' The *Richmond Herald* refers more specifically to a 'Joseph Owers', possibly a beer retailer in Fulham.[264] His wife had been born in Bath, so there is a possible link with Richardson there.

Frederick Owers, a year older than Tom, was Assistant Superintendent of the Poplar Insurance Company and played cricket for the Dundonald Club in Wimbledon. Tom's elder brother, Charles Henry, was an insurance agent, so there may have been a professional as well as a cricket connection. Newspapers are less than 100% accurate when it comes to initials, but the strong likelihood is that it is the same family involved and the locals in Aix-les-Bains and Saint Jean d'Arvey mistakenly assumed that they were part of Richardson's family. The *Sporting Life* has the family arriving in Chambéry from Aix-les-Bains on the morning of Thursday 4 July,[265] but as the telegram informing Richardson's own family of the death was being delivered in Richmond about the same time, this was almost certainly the Owers family. The Richardsons left for France on the same day.[266]

There are, however, factual contradictions between contemporary press evidence and Barker's account, based on correspondence with local officials and conversations with Tom Richardson's son and with Herbert

---

260   *Daily Tribune, Chicago* 8 November 1891: Mark Twain *Travel Letters*
261   *Ten Great Bowlers* p 125
262   15 July 1912
263   12 July 1912
264   *Census of Population* 1901
265   5 July 1912
266   *Richmond Herald* 6 July 1912

*Gorge and waterfall of Le Bout-du-Monde near where
Richardson's body was found.*

Strudwick. For instance, according to the latter two, Richardson was in
good health[267] just before he left for France whereas *The Times* reported
that he was seriously ill.[268] However, there is no evidence sufficiently
serious as to reopen the possibility of suicide.

Whether he was in the best or worst of health or somewhere in-between,
the local newspaper which reported his death records him as 'donnant des
signes d'aliénation mentale'[269] (showing signs of mental disorientation),
but has no hint of suicide and attributes the death to congestion.

> **Disparu**
> M. Richardson, un de nos hôtes an-
> glais, était descendu au Nicolas-Bar, il
> a disparu, donnant des signes d'aliéna-
> tion mentale.
>   Voici les dépêches publiées par le
> *Lyon* :
>   On vient de découvrir dans les gorges
> de la Leysse, entre La Corbière et Saint-
> Jean-d'Arvey, le cadavre d'un excursion-
> niste anglais, nommé John Richardson,
> habitant à Richemond-Green.
>   Le corps a été déposé dans une salle
> de la mairie, où il a été réclamé par
> la famille.
>   La mort paraît être attribuée à une
> congestion.

*Item in the local newspaper announcing the discovery of Richardson's body.
[L'Avenir d'Aix-les-Bains]*

The report in the local newspaper may be roughly translated as:

DISAPPEARED
Mr Richardson, one of our English guests, was staying at the Nicolas-
Bar: he went out showing signs of mental disorientation.

---

267   *Ten Great Bowlers* p 125
268   4 July 1912
269   *Avenir d'Aix-les-Bains* 6 July 1912

[Archive municipale d' Aix-les-Bains]

*The 'Nicolas-Bar' in the Rue du Casino in Aix-les-Bains, now L'Addict.
Tom Richardson spent his last days here.*

Dispatches from the *Lyon* read as follows:
The body of an English tourist John [sic] Richardson, a resident of
Richmond Green was found in the Leysse Gorge between la Corbière
and St Jean d'Arvey. It was kept in a room at the Town Hall and has
now been handed over to his family. Death was apparently caused by
congestion.

The 'Nicolas-Bar' is still there, though not under the same name. At the
time, the signs outside indicate that it was Nicola's Restaurant or Nicola's
American Bar, although it is not clear whether some one called Nicola was
involved or whether the name of the place arises simply from a Gallic
misunderstanding of the apostrophe. It was a modest establishment with a
few rooms to let and not in the same league as the adjacent Hotel du Nord
et Grande Bretagne. In between was an Institut de Beauté which covered
hairdressing, pedicure and massage services. The hotel is no longer such,

Immediately opposite is the Casino...

and adjacent, the plaques of doctors specialising in conditions which brought patients to the sulphur springs.

but a professional establishment, housing physicians whose specialisms relate to those where the Aix-les-Bains sulphur baths might contribute to a cure or alleviation, for example, sports medicine, rheumatology, osteopathy, physiotherapy etc. The Institut de Beauté has become a toy shop, but the concept continues in an upmarket beauty salon, part of the Nocibé chain, which is now housed in what was part of the hotel. The 'Nicolas-Bar' itself is now called l'Addict and is a lounge bar, according to the publicity outside, specialising in cocktails and Guinness. So the Anglophile flavour has been retained.

The report in the *Daily Mail*, probably from the same news agency, is consistent on the cause of death, but not on the time

Paris, Thursday 1 am

> The *Journal* has received a telegram from Aix-les-Bains announcing that Tom Richardson, the famous Surrey fast bowler was found dead yesterday morning at the foot of a hill by the village of St. Jean d'Arvey. Death was apparently due to cerebral congestion brought on by exposure.
>
> On Tuesday night, Richardson, according to the *Journal*, left his hotel without being observed by the nurses and his family. He went out in his slippers and without a tie or collar.[270]

The last paragraph is clearly incorrect. Whether he went out in his slippers and without collar and tie there is no way of knowing, but by Tuesday evening, he was already dead. According to the death certificate, an undertaker from Aix-les-Bains and a retired local gendarme discovered the body (The 'Disparu' headline in the local paper suggests that the alarm had been raised) and testified before the Mayor twenty-four hours later that the time of the discovery had been 3 pm on the afternoon of Tuesday 2nd.

Richardson must have had a passport and/or other identity papers on him, as the statement by the undertaker and gendarme gives his address and occupation correctly, as well as the name of his estranged wife. Under French Law, the declaration before the Mayor should be within twenty-four hours (which it was – just) by relatives or neighbours (which it wasn't – there weren't any around) and it should also be accompanied by a medical certificate. Again, it wasn't – the only instance in the St Jean d'Arvey registers – and no cause of death is given.

The *Evening News* the same day also carries the story. It is consistent to the extent that it also mentions that he went out without a tie or collar and wearing slippers and adds that he had 400 francs in his pocket. However, it has the time of his departure at 5 am, rather than the evening and the discovery of the body after the police had been alerted in the late evening rather than the next day. It was, in fact, much earlier.

How Tom came to be anywhere near St Jean d'Arvey is something of a mystery. True, according to Richardson's son, and confirmed by 'Felix'

---

270   4 July 1912

*The death certificate – in the judicial French of the early twentieth century.
An approximate English equivalent would be:*

3 July 1912   3 pm

*Before us, Marie-Antoinette d'Oncieu, acting as Registrar of Births, Marriages
and Deaths for the parish of St Jean d'Arvey in the North District of Chambéry
appeared, firstly, Marc Vuillermet, aged 52, Funeral Director at Aix-les-Bains and
secondly, Francois Duchatel, aged 49, retired gendarme of this parish, being
neither relatives nor neighbours of the deceased and declared that Jean[sic}
Richardson aged 42 years, publican at Richmond Green (Surrey, England)
whose descent we have been unable to trace, but whose mother and father are
deceased, estranged husband of the living Edith Emma Cheesman, died at
St Jean d'Arvey in an open field called "Les Molliennes"* on the second of July
of the present year at three o'clock in the afternoon, while passing through this
parish. Having confirmed the death, we immediately drew up and entered in the
two registers the death certificate which we have read to the informants who
have signed it along with us.*

M Vuillermet   *d'Oncieu*
F Duchatel   *Mayor*
* Mollière on current maps

when commenting on the loss of form in 1897/98, his father was in the habit of taking long walks, as evidenced by the myth, albeit exploded, that he walked regularly from Mitcham to The Oval. However, Aix-les-Bains is a good fifteen kilometres from the St Jean d'Arvey area. There is no direct road and to get there, even if he had initially taken the Aix-les-Bains – Chambéry road, he would at some stage have turned off into some attractive but inhospitable terrain. He would have found himself in the Leysse valley with mallards, pochards and kingfishers, between the Massifs of the Bauges to the north and the Chartreuse to the south, near a waterfall called Le Bout-du-Monde and a depression called Le Trou des Enfers, which, according to locals, are best avoided by ordinary pedestrians and left to experienced mountaineers. Perhaps, overweight, lost and disoriented, his mind and body could take no more.

Furthermore, wearing a collar and tie, even for informal occasions was a convention generally observed in the early twentieth century and their absence as well as wearing slippers for a long country walk may well be 'signes d'aliénation mentale', but they do not add up to preparation for suicide.

The *Sporting Life*, picked up the news a day after the *Daily Mail*, but along with *The Times* was seemingly more accurate in locating the place of Richardson's death at the Cascade du Bout-du-Monde and mentioned in addition that he had been taken ill in a café.

That he was taken ill in a café may well be correct, but savage irony as it might have been to end one's life in a place called the Bout-du-Monde – also a hamlet as well as a waterfall – the place where his body was found was in open country at a place called "les Molliennes" (Molliène on current maps) in the Chemin des Vignes, now forested but then open country with vines and peach trees. Enquiries made in St Jean d'Arvey have revealed that not even the most elderly residents with the sharpest memories can recall being told by parents or grandparents of the events of 2 and 3 July 1912.[271]

The location of the Nicolas-Bar may be of significance in piecing together the story of Tom Richardson's last hours. It is very convenient for the thermal baths, but even more so for the casino, being directly opposite. His job as a publican would mean that he was a late-night rather than an early-morning person, so it perhaps makes sense to see the 5 am departure as an extension of the previous day. Had he perhaps had a decent win at the casino, had a few drinks, removed his collar and tie, put on his slippers and wandered off for some fresh air?

The 400 francs found in his pocket is also something of a clue. It was a substantial sum of money. Statisticians and economists may well get their knickers in a twist over comparative purchasing power, but as a very rough guide, the local newspaper at the time cost 10 centimes, so

---

271   A little surprising perhaps: though the population of St Jean d'Arvey is just over 1,500, 1912 would be within the memory of many people's grandparents, if not their parents. My own grandmother was able to recall events that took place in that year, like the sinking of the *Titanic* and Barnsley winning the FA Cup.

The Leysse Valley.

The end of Saint Jean d'Arvey. It marked the end for Tom Richardson.
[Mairie et St Jean d'Arvey]

View of St Jean d'Arvey: "Molliene" is to the left.
Aix-les-Bains the other side of the mountain.
[Marie de St Jean d'Arvey]

the amount Richardson had with him would have bought 4,000 of them. More scientifically perhaps, there is a website on *inter alia* the purchasing power of the franc at different dates[272] which suggests 1 franc in 1912 would be equivalent to ₤3.1753. The tables are accompanied by a caveat that the figures may be less reliable for further distant periods and while tolerably accurate for domestic consumption, they are somewhat more fragile as a measure of inflation. Nevertheless, even allowing for all that and fluctuating exchange rates, it is safe to say that Tom's 400 francs can be valued at over £1,000 in today's money. It is a sum that most people would not take out with them.

Had he perhaps become hopelessly lost and dehydrated in the midsummer, midday heat (perhaps between 25 and 30° at that time of year)? Are the 'signes d'aliénation mentales' the euphemistic equivalent of being tired and emotional? His previously diagnosed heart condition may have also have been a contributory factor. It is all highly speculative and many pieces of the jigsaw are missing, but those that remain do begin to form a consistent and credible picture.

His family – press reports are not specific as to which members – were alerted by telegram and immediately travelled to Chambéry.[273]

It was a sad irony that the information reached England during 'Razor' Smith's benefit match. On the same front page that Richardson's death was announced, the *Sporting Life* reported:

---

272 Institut national de la statistique et des études économiques: Pouvoir d'achat de l'euro et du franc.
273 *Richmond Herald* 6 July 1912

THE PRINCE AND 'RAZOR'

In forwarding a cheque for £3 3s to W.C.('Razor') Smith yesterday, the Prince of Wales asked the Surrey bowler if he would let him know how it came about that the nickname 'Razor' was given him. Smith's own version is as follows: During a match many years ago, Tom Richardson (whose death by a sad coincidence is confirmed today) commented several times on Smith's leanness. He eventually remarked that he could not see Smith at all when he was standing sideways and added that if he were stropped once more he would be thin enough to shave with.[274]

Learning that there were insufficient funds to bring the body back to England, within a week the newspaper established a fund for the purpose of doing that and, in accordance with Richardson's own wishes, have him buried in the soil of his native county. Any residue would be used to establish a fund for Richardson's dependents. The response from individuals and commercial organisations was instant and generous. 'Razor' Smith was one of the first contributors and

Mr R.W.Inman touches the right note when he states in his letter: "Gladly I enclose my mite, and sorry am I that I cannot do more. I had the pleasure of seeing the splendid man play in many great matches, and I also had the gratification of seeing much of him during his proprietorship of the Prince's Head, and ever did I find him one of the best. Only a few days ago, I invited him to join me in a drink. Little did I imagine how near his end he was.[275]

Within a couple of days, however, St John Harmsworth, whose Perrier Water Company already headed the subscription list with a donation of £10, had agreed to meet the full costs of embalming, repatriating the body and the funeral, an eventual commitment of £133 2s 9d.

St John Harmsworth, in his mid-thirties at the time, had invested in the company of the mineral water spring at Vergèze. He renamed it 'Perrier' after Dr Louis Perrier who had started marketing the water in 1894. Harmsworth sold his share in the family newspaper business (his brothers became newspaper barons Lords Northcliffe and Rothermere) to buy the source and in 1906 formed *La Compagnie de la Source Perrier*. He was personally responsible for the distinctively shaped bottle based on the popular exercise clubs of the time which Harmsworth himself had used as part of his rehabilitation from an accident.

He wrote to the *Sporting Life* in the following terms:

Poynters Hall,
Totteridge,
Herts

To the Editor of the "Sporting Life"

Dear Sir

I have been following with very sympathetic interest your "Tom Richardson" fund.

---

274   5 July 1912

275   *Sporting Life* 9 July 1912

Without in any way wishing to take the place of the number of admirers of our greatest bowler and a fine gentleman, all over the country, who will most assuredly desire to contribute to this fund when the tragic circumstances of Tom Richardson's last days are brought home to them. I will personally, if there is any doubt about the necessary money being found, take upon myself all charges in connection with the bringing home of his body to England.

ST JOHN HARMSWORTH

The Editor replied immediately:

Gratefully accept your generous offer. Rest of subscriptions will be set apart for dependents.

EDITOR, "SPORTING LIFE"

but continued to press for funds for the dependents:

Tom Richardson will, therefore, have his wish granted: he will be buried in the land of his birth ...

The duty to the dead will now be carried out. What of the duty to the living? Tom Richardson, as we mentioned in our original appeal, has left several dependents, including three children, who are not old enough to earn their own livelihood. Let us repeat with all emphasis that Tom Richardson, although generous and kind-hearted was never prodigal of his substance, and such resources as he had were drained in recent years by ill-health.[276]

Later appeals drop any reference to the other dependents, but continue to mention the children. There is no mention of his widow. The coffin arrived at Victoria Station on the afternoon of Thursday 11 July and the funeral took place at Richmond two days later. In deference to Richardson's wishes, those attending were asked to wear 'complimentary' rather than 'deep' mourning. For one shortly past his fortieth birthday to express such a wish as well as stating where he wished to be buried suggests that he was well aware that his ill-health could lead to a premature death.

All the other donations went into a trust fund for the family. Surrey donated £50:[277] it is recorded in the Accounts for 1912, adjacent to an amount just 1/2 more for the hire and keep of a horse. There is no mention of Richardson in the annual report though the 'regrettable death' of a committee member features.[278] The eventual total of £174 included contributions from many of his former colleagues and fellow licensees in Richmond and 14/- from a whip-round in the public bar of the *Prince's Head*.

Corœbus of the *Morning Advertiser*, in a feature also reproduced in the local *Mitcham Advertiser*, gave an outstandingly complimentary tribute, and one which rarely for the period, (though the advent of the *Daily Mail* and the beginnings of tabloid journalism in the late nineteenth century, was

276   *Sporting Life* 11 July 1912
277   Surrey CCC minutes 18 July, 1 August and 5 September 1912
278   Surrey CCC Yearbook 1912 pp 55,58 and 59

becoming less rare) comments on lifestyle and the domestic background.

The news of Tom Richardson's tragic end came as a great shock to everyone interested in cricket. Though he had for some time dropped out of the game the once matchless bowler was in no sense forgotten. His deeds were too recent for that. In common with others behind the scenes I knew perfectly well that Richardson had for a considerable time past lived very unwisely, but I was not aware that his condition was such as to threaten any immediate danger. Indeed, the last time I saw him – about two months ago – he looked better than he had looked last year. It is sad to think of a man with his splendid physique being dead in his forty-second year. He ought to have lived to eighty. I fancy domestic trouble was his undoing, but I have very imperfect knowledge of the facts.

For consistent excellence as a fast bowler, Richardson had no equal in his time...[279]

The Times, not normally prone to exaggeration, had few doubts about Richardson's position in the fast bowling hierarchy:

No county in our time has had two such fast bowlers as Lockwood and Richardson at their best. The late George Freeman is often spoken of as the greatest of fast bowlers, but the wickets on which he played were for the most part inferior to those on which Richardson won his fame.[280]

Tom's obituary in *Cricket* a couple of weeks later, after rehearsing some of his statistical achievements, concludes by slightly misquoting *Hamlet* :

He was a man, take him for all in all,
We shall not look upon his like again.[281]

He left estate to the value of £629 and, says Tom Higgs, 'a host of memories for old Mitchamers'[282]

of which the net personalty has been sworn at £138. He left to his son Tom William Richardson to devolve, as heirlooms, the cricket balls presented to him during his cricket career and all his cricketing mementoes. [283]

The *Mitcham Advertiser* was not alone in its solemn and sober report of his funeral on the afternoon of Saturday 13 July:

Tom Richardson, who met his death in such tragic circumstances at Aix-les-Bains, was buried on Saturday at Richmond Cemetery. A large number of people – both along the route to the cemetery and at the grave-side – assembled to pay their last respects to the remains of the famous bowler. Starting from the Roman Catholic Church, the Vineyard, shortly after three o'clock, the cortege reached the burial

279   *Mitcham Advertiser* 12 July 1912
280   4 July 1912
281   20 July 1912
282   *Mitcham C C Yearbook* 1989
283   *Times* 29 August 1912 under 'Wills and Bequests'

ground about four o'clock.

W.Richardson and C.Richardson, brothers of the deceased, were the chief mourners, and amongst those who followed were several of Richardson's colleagues in the old Mitcham team in which he first made his name as a bowler. Several well-known cricketers of the present and past generations were present including H.Strudwick, W.C.Smith, G.Platt, T.Rushby, R.Abel, H.Wood, W.Brockwell and A.Chester. Among others were W.G.East (King's bargemaster), A.André (representing the Richmond hospital), H.Rockett (secretary, Richmond Athletic Grounds) A.S.Bull, Peter Lees (green-keeper, mid-Surrey Golf Club), Col. J.Leslie Powell, Ernest Howard (solicitor to the deceased). H.Strutt-Cavell, T.P.Harvey, A.F.Clarke, F.Knight and J.Caffarey (Mitcham CC).

The wreaths were numerous and beautiful, close upon 50 being sent. The Surrey County Club sent one, as did the Surrey professionals (a broken wicket), the professionals at Lords [sic] and the gentlemen playing in the match at the Oval. This bore the inscription: "In affectionate regard to the memory of a warm-hearted friend and comrade." Others were sent by H.Wood, Robert Henderson, Walter Lees, Mr and Mrs G.W.Ayres, C.E.Green, Mrs Luff, Mr and Mrs W.G.East, A.E.Stoddart, H.D.G.Leveson Gower, W.Brockwell, Mitcham CC and a few old cricketing friends in Mitcham. Many of the wreaths were tied with the coloured ribbons of clubs and teams for which Richardson had played.[284]

The grave was lined with ivy and flowers, provided at no charge by a local florist and among the fifty wreaths was one from Lizzie, the local flower seller. [285]

It is not clear what happened to the fund. It was raised in a Surrey committee meeting seven years later in 1919 and the Secretary was instructed to pursue enquiries. However,

The Secretary reported the negative results of the enquiries so far made. It was decided that no further action be taken. [286]

None was: or at least, if it was, it was not recorded in the minutes. Tom Richardson and his memories had passed into history:

TOM RICHARDSON

Golden heart, lion heart, Surrey's stalwart son,
   Passed untimely to the distant bourne.
The flag is flying half-mast high at famous Kennington.
   Comrades of the old days for you mourn.

Great heart, high heart, warrior unsubdued –
   Not since Surrey's Walter paid the debt,
Debt we all in turn must pay, hath Surrey ever rued
   Any loss like yours – we'll not forget!

---

284   *Mitcham Advertiser* 19 July 1912
285   *Richmond Herald* 27 July 1912
286   Surrey CCC minutes 18 December 1919.

Tom, we'll not forget you –we'll remember days of yore,
  Sweltering days of July heat on Old Trafford ground,
When the wondrous Rajput Prince topped the English score,
  When for fight heroic waged man made your praise resound,

Fast on many a summer day crashed the wickets down
  Before the battery of your swift attack.
Soon green turf shall cover you, bowler of high renown,
  Rest in peace, Tom – mourners you'll not lack.[287]

*Tom Richardson's grave in Richmond Cemetery. He rests there alone, neither
his widow nor his family joining him in later years.*

287   *Cricket* 13 July 1912

TOM RICHARDSON.

MORE MONEY NEEDED FOR THE FUND.

TO-DAY'S FUNERAL.

It is the intention of Mr. W. Lotinga to arrange a benefit match for the Tom Richardson fund. Meanwhile much more money is needed. It will be set aside for the benefit of the three children who are left.

Tom Richardson is to be buried to-day. He will be laid to rest at Richmond, where he lived so long. The cortege will start from opposite the Roman Catholic Church, The Vineyard, at 3.15, and the cemetery will be reached about 4 o'clock. The route is as follows:—

Hill Rise.   George-street.
Hill-street.   Sheen-road.
        Queen's-road.

That there will be a big attendance to do honour to the passing of a great sportsman is certain. It is well known that Tom Richardson had well-defined wishes in the matter of mourning, and out of deference to his views, those who attend are asked to wear complimentary, rather than deep, mourning. Councillor G. W. Heasler, of Richmond, has the arrangements in hand, and any wreaths may be sent to the Prince's Head, Richmond Green.

The match at the Oval to-day will be stopped at ten minutes to four until ten minutes past four. That is the time when the cortege will have reached the cemetery.

Mr. St. John Harmsworth has very generously undertaken to defray the cost of the funeral, so that the money sent into the fund will all go towards the maintenance, &c., of the children. There are three of them, all too young to yet earn their own livelihood, and it is for them that we continue our appeal. Those who contribute are, by so doing, honouring the memory of one of the greatest fast bowlers the world has known, and at the same time making it possible that the after lives of those he has left behind will be free from financial care.

The response so far has been good, but much more money is required. For the dead, all that could be done has been done; it is the living who now call for attention.

Yesterday Mr J. S. Walker suggested that a big benefit match should be arranged. We cordially endorsed the suggestion, and now we have to record that a movement is on foot to bring the idea to fruition. We have received a wire from Mr W. Lotinga, in which he says that he proposes to organise a benefit match on a big and unique scale. His plan is to have one side composed of sporting notabilities, who will be opposed by the Surrey team. Nothing has as yet been definitely arranged, or course, for Mr Lotinga has not had time to see either the Surrey players or the committee. But we feel certain that they will at once agree. Those who remember the football match arranged by Mr Lotinga last winter will not need to be told of its success from every standpoint. There are great possibilities in such a cricket match as this.

Mr A. Woodward, in sending on a cheque for £5, suggests that collections should be made at all county cricket grounds.

As already stated, there is a need for considerably more money. Further subscriptions will be immediately acknowledged by the Editor of the "Sporting Life," 27, St. Bride-st., E.C., or Mr Strutt-Cavell, 14, Napoleon-rd., Twickenham.

The list to date is as follows:—

	£	s.	d.
Perrier Water Co.	10	0	0
Surrey Club Professionals (per Ernie Hayes)	10	0	0
Proprietor of "Sporting Life"	5	5	0
"Gale's Special"	5	5	0
Golf Illustrated, Ltd.	2	2	0
Mr A. L. Ayer	2	2	0
Mr Dick Depledge	2	2	0
Mr J. Mears, Old Ship Hotel, Richmond	1	1	0
Mr F. H. Huish	1	1	0
"A Right and Left" at Hatherden	1	1	0
Mr W. J. P. Stephens	1	1	0
Mr Tom Woodbury	1	1	0
Mr John S. Walker	1	1	0
Mr A. Walker, South-Western Hotel, Richmond	1	1	0
Mr J. T. Hearne	1	1	0
Mr A. G. Whiteman	1	1	0
Mr F. Chas. Gamble	1	1	0
A Few Surreyites (per Mr H. A. Williams)		17	0
Mr Frank H. Headicar		10	0
The Editor of "Cricket"		10	0
R. G. D.		5	0
Mr C. W. Fox		5	0
A Surrey Man		5	0
Mr Chas. F. Barwell		5	0
Mr Ernest E. Moss		5	0
C. T.		5	0
Standlake		2	6
Petersham		2	6
Per Mr Strutt-Cavell :—			
Mr C. J. Kohler	5	5	0
Mr W. Lotinga	1	1	0
Mr Frank Tarrant (Middlesex)	1	1	0
Mr Wilfrid Rhodes (Yorkshire)	1	1	0
Mr W. C. ("Razor") Smith	1	0	0
Mr Robt. W. Inman	1	0	0
Mr Will Osborne		10	6
Mr J. T. Ayres		10	0
Mr Con Egan		10	6
H. F. G. S.		10	0
Mr J. E. Groome (Clapham)		5	0
Mr Bob Clouting (Richmond)		5	0
Mr S. M. Philip (Richmond)		5	0
Mr Joe Millett (Sun Inn Richmond)		5	0
Mr Maurice Read		5	0
Mr Jim Knowles (Mortlake)		5	0
Mr Geo. Robinson (Richmond)		5	0
Mr Tom H. Toon (Richmond)		5	0
Mr W. H. Ord (Richmond)		5	0
Mr H. Hambler (Richmond)		5	0
Mr S. J. Dickson (Honor Oak C.C.)		5	0
Mr W. Irving (Richmond)		5	0
Mr Geo. Eydmann (Richmond)		2	6
Per Mr Tom Ratcliff (First List) :—			
Mr W. G. East	1	0	0
Dr F. Wadd		10	0
Tom Ratcliff		10	0
Mr G. W. Heasler		10	0
Mr W Hiorns		10	0
Mr J. E. Shrubsole		10	0
Sir Thos. Skewes Cox		10	0
Mr C Cornell		10	0
Dr Taylor		5	0
Mr Arthur Jiggins		5	0
Mr A. J. Wheatley		5	0
Mr J J Bisgood		2	6
J. H. C.		2	6
Per Mr Alf Woodward, Wandsworth Common :—			
Alf Woodward 10s., J Walsh 10s., F Maddox 10s., Ted Robinson 10s., Bert Yorke 5s., E. Hulin 5s., S. Errington 5s., A. T. 5s., C. Smith 5s., Bob and Mel 5s., J. T. 5s., W. Lindley 5s., C. Newnham 5s., J. Pearce 2s. 6d., W. Prince 2s. 6d., A. Klass 2s. 6d., E. Slingsby 2s. 6d., T. Eldridge 2s. 6d., Horace 2s., A. M. and G. 2s., Make Up 1s.	5	0	0
Ernie Barry's Training Camp (per Mr Ernest Barry)	0	10	0

Report giving details of funeral and subscription list for the Sporting Life Fund.
[Sporting Life 13 July 1912]

Appendix A
Career Statistics

Statistics and milestones are relevant only within the context of the situation of the game. Otherwise the compilation of hundreds and five-fers is pointless because it becomes an end in itself, oblivious to those playing and watching. It demonstrates a lack of respect, which is surely at the heart of what is called the Spirit of Cricket. [1]

All very true. In Richardson's case it was a question of hundreds *of* five-fers (well, two anyway) rather than hundreds *and* five-fers and although there may have been a few in 'dead' or festival matches, the vast majority were achieved in pursuit of victory for Surrey, England or any representative team in which he featured.

Trans-generational comparisons can be futile because of very different playing conditions. In the nineteenth century the usually uncovered pitches were less friendly to batsmen and tail-enders were not expected to contribute much with the bat. Consequently totals were lower and there were many instances of an opening bowler (often both) being kept on through a much shorter innings with the result that the proportion of wickets taken, compared with those taken by change bowlers was higher than it is today. Given those caveats and recognising that although statistics never reveal everything it is rare that they reveal nothing and some of Richardson's are so spectacular that they stood out in his own generation and remain memorable today.

1. Test Matches

	O	M	R	W	BB	Ave	5wl	10wM
1893	67.4 (a)	20	156	10	5-49	15.60	2	1
1894-95	291.2 (b)	63	849	32	6-104	26.53	4	-
1896	175.1 (a)	58	439	24	7-168	18.29	4	2
1897-98	255.5 (b)	50	776	22	8-94	35.27	1	1
	243 (a)							
	547.1 (b)	191	2220	88	8-94	25.22	11	4

Economy Rate 2.96 (per 6 ball equivalent)
Strike Rate 51.11

All First-class Matches

	O	M	R	W	BB	Ave	5wl	10wM
1892	234.3 (a)	77	602	29	5-43	20.75	1	-
1893	993.4 (a)	288	2680	174	9-47	15.40	20	7
1894	933.4 (a)	291	2024	196	10-45	10.32	22	11

---

1   Mike Atherton *The Times* 7 July 2011

Season	Overs		Runs	Wickets	Best	Average		
1894-95 (Aus)	592 (b)	148	1616	68	8-52	23.76	7	1
1895	1691.1 (a)	463	4170	290	9-49	14.37	36	17
1896	1657.2 (a)	526	4015	246	8-82	16.32	26	10
1897	1603.4 (a)	496	3945	273	8-49	14.45	34	13
1897-98 (Aus)	524.2 (b)	107	1593	54	8-94	29.50	4	1
1898	1223.4 (a)	340	3147	161	8-28	19.54	12	4
1899	1017.1 (a)	281	2505	98	6-60	25.56	4	-
1900	16 (a)							
	983.5(b)	241	2949	122	8-90	24.17	8	3
1901	1293.4(b)	271	3697	159	7-89	23.25	10	1
1902	884.1(b)	172	2607	106	7-53	24.59	6	1
1903	928 (b)	193	2732	119	7-57	22.95	10	3
1904	131.1 (b)	18	446	9	3-73	49.55	-	-
1905	13 (b)	1	65	-			-	-
	9371.3 (a)							
	5350.1 (b)	3913	38793	2104	10-45	18.43	200	72

Economy Rate 2.94 (per 6 ball over equivalent)
Strike Rate 37.52
5 ball overs (a)
6 ball overs (b)

2. Records once held

Most wickets in a season
290 in 1895. It was passed by A P Freeman in 1928.
Most wickets in four consecutive seasons
1005 (1894/97) again eclipsed by Freeman with 1122 (1928/31)
He had 2104 first-class wickets, third at the time to W G Grace and Johnny Briggs.
He stands 24th in the all-time list.

3. Records for Surrey still held

Nine or more wickets in an innings on four occasions
10-45 v Essex (The Oval) 1894; 9-47 v Yorkshire (Bramall Lane) 1893;
9-49 v Sussex (The Oval) 1895; 9-70 v Hampshire (The Oval) 1895.
No one else has achieved the feat as many times; Lockwood has three, Loader,
Lock and Bicknell two each and ten others once each.
Ten or more wickets in a match on sixty occasions
Lohmann is next with 41.
Most wickets (1775)
There are fifteen players who have taken over 1,000 wickets, Lock being next on
the list with 1,713, Martin Bicknell the most recent (and almost certainly the last)
with 1,026.
Most wickets at The Oval (927)
Lock is next with 821.
Most wickets in a season
252 in 1895; 238 in 1897; 202 in 1896; 196 in 1894.
Only W C Smith has more than 200 (225 in 1910)

Most wickets in a season at The Oval
123 in 1895; 122 in 1896; 106 in 1897. W.C.Smith is next with 104 in 1910.
Most consecutive five-wicket innings (7)
In 1897: Southerton is next with six in 1871 and 1873.
Richardson also had six in 1895 and 1897.
Most consecutive matches with five wickets in an innings (17)
Also in 1897: Lohmann is next with 13 in 1888-1889.
Most hat-tricks (4)
v Gloucestershire (The Oval) 1893.
v Leicestershire (The Oval) 1896.
v Sussex (The Oval) 1898.
v Warwickshire (The Oval) 1898.
Forty-six instances in all (including four of four in four balls). Lockwood and Laker had three each.

4. Distribution of Wickets in 1895

The majority of Tom Richardson's wickets were gained by hitting the stumps. Had the 1935 lbw law been introduced half-a century earlier he would doubtless have had more than 2,104 first-class wickets and a higher proportion would have been gained in this way. His record-breaking season of 1895 when he took 290 wickets was fairly typical, well over half being bowled. A comparison with the wickets taken by swing and seam bowlers in the first half of Surrey's 2011 LV Championship season indicates how the game has changed.

	Richardson 1895	Surrey 2011
Bowled	176 (61%)	37 (20%)
LBW	6 (2%)	34 (19%)
Caught by wicket-keeper	31 (11%)	48 (26%)
Caught elsewhere	67 (23%)	62 (34%)
Caught and bowled	9 (3%)	2 (1%)
Hit wicket	1	
	----------------	------------
	290	183
	=========	========

Appendix B
Family Tree

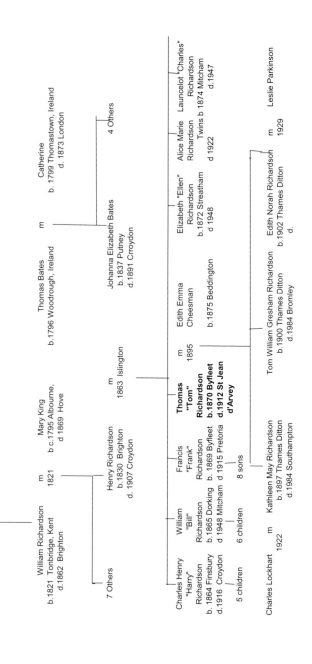

Appendix C1

First-Class Cricketers in the Richardson family

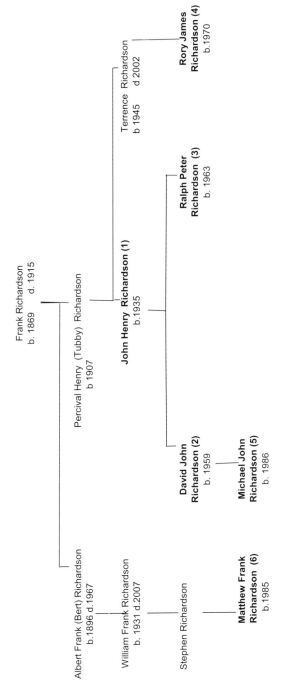

Frank Richardson
b. 1869   d. 1915

Percival Henry (Tubby) Richardson
b 1907

Terrence Richardson
b 1945   d 2002

Rory James
Richardson (4)
b.1970

John Henry Richardson (1)
b.1935

Ralph Peter
Richardson (3)
b. 1963

David John
Richardson (2)
b. 1959

Michael John
Richardson (5)
b. 1986

Albert Frank (Bert) Richardson
b.1896 d.1967

William Frank Richardson
b. 1931 d.2007

Stephen Richardson

Matthew Frank
Richardson (6)
b.1985

Appendix C2

... and their Playing Records

William Thayer's biography of assassinated President James Garfield was entitled *Log Cabin to White House.* If the mythology of the Romany origins of the Richardson family were to be believed, then the equivalent – albeit over four generations – would perhaps be *From Gypsy Caravan to ICC*, Tom's great-great nephew, David, after a distinguished international playing career, being General Manager - Cricket of the International Cricket Council. None of Tom's immediate family – a son and two daughters – was involved in cricket, but the genes have worked through the generations and a number of his indirect descendants, all from his elder brother, Frank who settled in South Africa, have played the game at a senior level. They are identified on the preceding 'Cricketers' Family Tree' and their career records are outlined below.

J.H.Richardson (1)
North Eastern Transvaal, Transvaal B
First-Class Batting and Fielding (1952/53-1960/61)

M	I	NO	R	HS	A	50	Ct	St
22	42	3	785	72	20.12	4	41	7

D.J.Richardson (2)
Eastern Province, Eastern Province B, Northern Transvaal, South Africa, South African Defence Force, South African Universities
Test Batting and Fielding (1991/92-1997/98)

M	I	NO	R	HS	A	100	50	SR	Ct	St
42	64	8	1359	109	24.26	1	8	41.93	150	2

First-Class Batting and Fielding (1977/78-1997/98)

M	I	NO	R	HS	A	100	50	Ct	St
200	310	51	6981	134	26.95	6	37	579	40

First-Class Bowling (1997/98)

O	M	R	W	Econ
1	0	3	0	3.00

One-Day International Batting and Fielding (1991/92-1997/98)

M	I	NO	R	HS	A	50	SR	Ct	St
122	77	33	868	53	19.72	1	66.87	148	17

One-Day Batting and Fielding (1979/80-1997/98)

M	I	NO	R	HS	A	50	Ct	St
280	214	69	3413	94	23.53	14	315	29

R.P.Richardson (3)
Western Province; Western Province B
First-Class Batting and Fielding (1984/85-1988/89)

M	I	NO	R	HS	A	50	Ct
10	17	4	181	52*	13.92	1	7

First-Class Bowling (1984/85-1988/89)

O	M	R	W	BB	A	E
173	27	521	10	3-23	52.10	3.01

One-Day Batting and Fielding (1988/89)

M	I	Ct
1	0	1

One-Day Bowling (1988/89)

O	M	R	W	E
3	0	13	0	4.33

R.J.Richardson (4)
Northern Transvaal, Northern Transvaal B
First-Class Batting and Fielding (1993/94)

M	I	NO	R	HS	A	Ct
1	1	0	5	5	5.00	3

One-Day Batting and Fielding (1992/93)

M	I
1	0

M.J.Richardson (5)
Durham
First-Class Batting and Fielding (2010-2011)

M	I	NO	R	HS	A	50	SR	Ct	St
5	7	1	161	73*	26.83	2	54.02	4	1

Michael Richardson was the ACS 2nd XI Cricketer of the Year for 2010. In the Championship he scored 562 runs at an average of 70.25 and in the Trophy 119 for once out in six innings. Additionally, following in his father's footsteps as a wicket-keeper, he had 30 catches and 2 stumpings in the Championship, 10 and 2 in the Trophy.

M.F.Richardson (6)
Border
First-Class Batting and Fielding (2006/07-2009/10)

M	I	NO	R	HS	A	50	SR	Ct
13	25	1	609	70	25.37	3	34.68	10

First-Class Bowling (2006/07)

O	M	R	W	E
1	0	3	0	3.00

One-Day Batting and Fielding (2005/06-2009/10)

M	I	NO	R	HS	A	50	SR	Ct
16	16	0	438	69	27.37	4	60.49	2

Terrence played one non-first-class match for the Northern Transvaal against South African Universities in 1968.

Appendix D
Chronology

1870	Born in Byfleet
c1875	Family moves to Mitcham
1889	(possibly before) Plays for Mitcham Cricket Club
1890	Signs as professional for Surrey
1892	Début for Surrey
1893	Début for England
1894/95	Tours Australia with A.E.Stoddart's team
1895	Takes 290 first-class wickets – a record which stood until 1928 - awarded 'star contract'
	Marries Edith Cheesman, moves to Thames Ditton and joins Thames Ditton Cricket Club
1896	Part of players' 'strike' for doubled Test match fee
1897/98	Again tours Australia with A.E.Stoddart's team; last Test Match
1899	Benefit year
1901	Takes tenancy of the *Cricketers* at Kingston
1904	Last season for Surrey
1905	Moves to Bath and takes tenancy of the *Wine Vaults*
	Last first-class match
1907	Returns to Surrey and takes tenancy of *Prince's Head* on Richmond Green
1908	(or before) Separates from Edith and lives with Emily Birch
1912	Dies at St Jean d'Arvey, France. Buried in Richmond Cemetery
1928/31	A.P.Freeman breaks Richardson's record for number of wickets in a season and over four consecutive seasons

Acknowledgements

A number of people and organisations have provided various levels of assistance, some substantial, in the provision of information for and the production of this book. My sincere thanks go to all of them.

Archives départementales de Savoie, Chambéry;

Archives municipales d'Aix-les-Bains;

Bath Central Library and Record Office, Bath and North East Somerset Council

British Newspaper Library;

HM Courts and Tribunals Service – Probate Sub-Registry;

London Borough of Merton Local Studies Library;

Richmond Local Studies Library;

Mairie de St Jean d'Arvey;

Surrey Cricket Library;

Surrey History Centre;

Graham Ashton, historian of Thames Ditton Cricket Club, for access to Club minutes and scorebooks, now deposited in the Surrey History Centre in Woking;

Martin Bicknell for finding time to contribute a Foreword on top of his strenuous training efforts for a triathlon;

Carol Davies Foster, Local Studies, Children's & Cultural Services, London Borough of Richmond upon Thames for access to local press items on Richardson's funeral;

Andrée Dussert, service des archives départementales de Savoie, for press items on Richardson's death at St Jean d'Arvey;

Charles Fellows-Smith for introducing me to John Lazenby's book on Jack Mason;

David Frith for supplying and allowing the use of the photographs of the balls with which Richardson took 10-45 against Essex in 1894 and 8-94 in his final Test match against Australia in 1898;

Sarah Gould, Heritage Officer, London Borough of Merton, for access to the records and photographs of Mitcham Cricket Club;

Derek and Betty Hambrook, residents of Commonside East, Mitcham, for their local knowledge of Mitcham in general and Hancock's Cottages in particular;

Margaret Griffiths, Heritage Public Services, Surrey History Centre;

Philip Harper, Archives Assistant, Bath Record Office, for information on Tom Richardson's time as landlord of the *Wine Vaults* in Bath;

David Harker and Andrew Titmus, Durham County Cricket Club;

David Jeater, series editor, for his interest and encouragement throughout the project and for proof reading;

Hélène McCann for her help with an article in French for *Le Sangerain*, the village magazine of St Jean d'Arvey;

Arthur Melville-Brown, President of the Cricket Philatelic Society, for the portraits of the 1897/98 tourists;

Jo Miller, Librarian, Surrey County Cricket Club, for her never-failing helpfulness in providing access to the Club Library, including photographs and museum items;

Roger Moulton for his conscientious and constructive editing;

Jenny Moulton for her proofreading;

Philip Paine for directing my attention to Richardson's grave in Richmond cemetery;

David Oram for locating press-cuttings relating to Richardson's death;

David Richardson, General Manager - Cricket, International Cricket Council, for information on the family and for contributing a Foreword;

Mary Lynn Richardson, great-niece of Tom Richardson, for access to her detailed research into family history, including reminiscences on an idyllic trip on the St Mawes ferry on a beautiful early Spring Cornish day;

Richard Shaw and all at City Press in Leeds for efficient and professional type-setting;

Tony Smith, friend of the Richardson family, for drawing my attention to Richardson memorabilia, particularly the diary of the 1897/98 tour of Australia;

Duncan Stone, University of Huddersfield Cricket Research Centre, for directing my attention (via David Frith) to the 1902 New Malden speech;

Marie-José Soubies, Deputy Mayor of St Jean d'Arvey, for her warm welcome to the village and providing a copy of Tom Richardson's death certificate as well as invaluable information on the geography of the area ;

Simon Sweetman for drawing my attention to Ben Travers' comment on Richardson's alcoholic consumption;

Iain Taylor for helping to identify the players in the photograph of the Surrey team of 1896;

Donald and Peter Van Rooyer, great-great-nephews of Tom, for family sporting reminiscences;

John Whitmore, former Secretary, Mitcham Cricket Club;

David Wood, Somerset County Cricket Club;

Peter Wynne-Thomas for access to his index of *The Cricketer;*

and, not least, my wife Jennifer for her never less than assiduous research into the Richardson family, Tom's life outside cricket and substantial help with the illustrations.

Sutton
Surrey
June 2012

Bibliography

Newspapers and periodicals

Annals of Sporting
The Australasian
L'Avenir d'Aix-les-Bains
Bath Chronicle
The Boy's Own Paper
Cricket, A Weekly Record of the Game
The Cricketer
Journal of the Cricket Society
Croydon Chronicle and East Surrey Advertiser
Daily Express
Daily Mail
Daily Telegraph
Daily Tribune, Chicago
The Guardian
London Review
Mid-Surrey Gazette
Mitcham Advertiser
Morning Chronicle
Nature
New York Times
Richmond Herald
Richmond and Twickenham Times
Le Sangerain
Sporting Life
Sunday Telegraph
Surrey Comet
Surrey Independent
Sydney Referee
The Times
Wimbledon Times

Books etc

Alverstone, Lord & Alcock, C.W. *Surrey Cricket: Its History and Associations* Longmans, Green and Co 1902

Arlott, John, *Fred: Portrait of a Fast Bowler* Eyre & Spottiswoode 1971

Ashton, Graham, *Thames Ditton Cricket Club: The First One Hundred and Fifty Years 1833-1983* Thames Ditton C C 1983

Aublet, Robert, *Nouveau Guide de Généalogie* Ouest France 1986

Bailey, Philip, Thorne, Philip, Wynne-Thomas, Peter, *Who's Who of Cricketers* Guild Publishing 1984

Barker, Ralph, *Ten Great Bowlers* Chatto & Windus 1967

Bettesworth, W.A., *Chats on the Cricket Field* Merritt and Hatcher 1910

Booth, Keith, *The Father of Modern Sport: The Life and Times of Charles W. Alcock* Parrs Wood Press 2002

Booth, Keith, *George Lohmann: Pioneer Professional* SportsBooks 2007

Cardus, Neville, *A Cricketer's Book* Grant Richards Ltd 1922

Cardus, Neville, *Six Giants of the Wisden Century* Wisden 1963

Clayton, Howard, [ed] *First-Class Counties Second Eleven Annual 2011*

ACS 2011

Colbourne, Pat, [ed] *Bath Cricket Club 1859-2009: 150 Years of Playing Cricket* Ralph Allen Press 2009

Cowley, Brian,[ed] *First-Class Records 1846-2000* Surrey CCC 2001

Dobbs, Brian, *Edwardians at play: Sport 1890-1914* Pelham Books 1973

Edmonds, Phil, *100 Greatest Bowlers* Macdonald Queen Anne Press 1989

Fingleton, J.H., *The Immortal Victor Trumper* Collins 1978

Francis, Tom, [edited by Eric Montague] *Old Mitcham* Phillimore & Co Ltd 1993

Frith, David, *The Fast Men* Van Nostrand Reinhold 1975

Frith, David, *The First Great Test Series 1894-1895* Queen Anne Press 1994

Frith, David, *Caught England, Bowled Australia* Eva Press 1997

Fry, C.B. *Life Worth Living* Eyre & Spottiswoode 1939

Giffen, George, *With Bat and Ball* Ward Lock and Co 1898

Harries, David, *Thames Ditton Cricket Club 1883-2008: Men in White on Giggs Hill Green* Thames Ditton C C 2008

Higgs, Tom, *300 Years of Mitcham Cricket* Malden Manor Press 1985

Higgs, Tom *Did Tom Richardson really walk to the Oval?* Mitcham CC Yearbook 1989

Hunter, David, *Tom Richardson: A Brief but Brilliant Ascendancy* The Cricketer July 1989

Laughton, Tony, *Captain of the Crowd: Albert Craig, Cricket and Football Rhymester* Boundary Books 2008

Lazenby, John, *Test of Time: Travels in Search of a Cricketing Legend* John Murray 2005

Leveson Gower, Sir Henry, *Off and On the Field* Stanley Paul 1953

James Lillywhite's Cricketers' Annual Lillywhite, Frowd & Co

McKinstry, Leo, *Jack Hobbs: the World's Greatest Cricketer* Yellow Jersey Press 2011

Mitcham Cricket Club Yearbooks

Montague, Eric, *Mitcham – A Pictorial History* Phillimore & Co Ltd 1991

Montague, Eric, *The Cricket Green* Merton Historical Society 2001

Post Office Bath Directories 1905-1908 William Lewis & Son

Rae, Simon, *W.G.Grace: A Life* Faber and Faber 1998

Ranjitsinhji, K.S., *With Stoddart's Team in Australia* James Bowden 1898

Robson, W., *Twentieth Century Britain* Oxford University Press 1983

Sandiford, Keith A.P., *Cricket and the Victorians* Scolar Press 1994

Sissons, Ric, *The Players* Kingswood Press 1988

Strudwick, Herbert, *25 Years Behind the Stumps* Hutchinson & Co Ltd 1926

Surrey CCC Yearbooks

Tellier, Laurence, *Aix en Savoie: hier et aujourd'hui* La Fontaine de Siloé 2009

Twain, Mark, *Travel Letters* Daily Tribune, Chicago 1891/92

Twigg, John, *Fast Bowling and Intimidation* Journal of the Cricket Society Autumn 1991 and Spring 1992

Whimpress, Bernard, *Ernie Jones; Australia's First Fast Bowler* [Lives in Cricket No. 4] ACS 2007

Wilde, Simon, *Number One: The World's Best Batsmen and Bowlers* Victor Gollancz 1998

Wilkins, Brian, *Cricket: The Bowler's Art* Kangaroo Press 1997

Wisden Cricketers Almanack

Woodcock, John, *One Hundred Greatest Cricketers* Macmillan 1998

Censuses of Population for 1871, 1881, 1891, 1901 and 1911

Websites etc

Ancestry, Cricket Archive, Legside Filth, Measuring Worth, Merton Historical Society, Mitcham Cricket Club, Science Museum – History of Medicine, Surrey County Cricket Club, Thames Ditton Cricket Club, Wikipedia

Index

A page number in bold indicates an illustration.

Abel, Bobby 22, 42, 47, **50**, 54, 55, 74, 76, **79**, 120
Adelaide 35, 38, 39, 66, 67
Ainslie, Ian 12,
Aix-les-Bains 12, 107, 108, 110, 112, 113, 114, 116, 119
Alcock, Charles W. 11
Ale House, Bath 91, **93**
all ten 30, 31, 60
Alston Cottages 13
Alverstone, Lord 86
Ambrose, Curtly 22
Anderson, Jimmy 64
André, A. 120
Andover 51, 52
Angel public house 48
Angel Road 48
Apted, Sam 74, 100
Armidale 35, 40
Arlott, John 95
Armitage, Tom 105
Armstrong, Warwick 92
Ashes 55, 64
Ashford (Middlesex) CC 94
Ashley-Cooper, F S 61, 86
Atherton, Mike 123
Attewell, William 100
Australia 22, 27, 28, 30, 33, 35-41, 47, 51, 52, 53, 55, 56, 57, 61, 64-71, 75, 77,92, 94, 96, 99 – 101, 105, 108
Ayres, George **29, 32**, 42, 48, **50**
Ayres , Mr and Mrs G. 119

Baggs, Thomas 91
Bailey's Magazine 16
Baldwin, Charles 42
Bale, E. 16
Ballarat 35
Bannermann, Alex 28
Basingstoke 52
Barbarians 97
Barker, Ralph 8, 13, 15, 56, 107, 108
Barnes, Sydney 7, 56
Barrington, Ken 15
Bates, Catherine (grandmother) 8, 125
Bates, Thomas (grandfather) 8, 125
Bates, Johanna (see 'Richardson')
Bath 91 – 96, 108
Bath and District 92
Bath Association Cricket Club 92
Bath Cricket Club 94
Bath Cricket Week 92
Bath Recreation Ground 6, 94
Bean, George 73
Beaumont, John 21

Beckenham 60
Bedfordshire 19
belle époque 107
Bendigo 35, 65
Bettesworth, W.A. 18, 46, 100
Bicknell, Martin 6, 124, 131
Birch, Emily ('Housekeeper') 88, 96
Blackham, J.M. 37
Board, Jack 75
Borradaile, O. R. 18
Botham, Ian 37
Bout-du-Monde **109**, 107 - 122
Bowley, Tom 21
Boyington, Fred **50**
Bracher, Frederick 43
Bradford 43
Bradman, Sir Donald 7
Bramall Lane, Sheffield 28, 89
Brann, George 73
Braund, Len **32**, 48, 89, 94,
Briggs, Johnny 28, 35, **36**, 37, 39, 40, 58, 65, **67**, 71, 75, 77, 124
Brighton 82, 89
Brisbane 35, 37, 40, 69,
Brockwell, William 27, 28, **29**, 30, 33, **36**, 37, 39, 40, 42, 48, 50, 61, 74, **79**, 86, 120
Brown, John T. **36**, 40
Browne, Royman 95
Bruce, William 28
Buckland, E.H. 21
Bull, A. S. 120
Bull, F.G. 58
Burns, James 12
Byfleet 8, 9, 11, 21, 61

Caddick, Andrew 6
Caffarey, J. 120
Cambridge University 21, 23, 27, 30, 72
Cardus, Neville 52 - 54, 99, 100
Carpenter, Herbert 60
casino, Aix-les-Bains **111**, 107 - 114
Catford Bridge 31, 43, 53
Ceylon 35
Chambéry 108, 113, 114, 116
Chatterton, William 23, 25
Cheesman, Charles (father-in-law) 9
Cheesman, Edith (see 'Richardson')
Cheesman, Emma 9, 11
Cheesman, Hannah (wife's aunt) 11
Chester, A. 120
Chesterfield 73
Clarke, A.F. 24, 120
Clifton College 28, 102
Coles, Percival 97

Colts (Surrey) 18
Commonside East, Mitcham 9, 13
Coe, Samuel 51
contract negotiations 89-90
County Championship 24, 29, 31, 45, 46, 56, 60, 77
Cowen, Margaret 12
Craig, Albert 24, 61, 91, 97
Crawford, V.F.S. **79**
Cricketers Inn, Kingston 83, **84**, 88, 91
Crossland, John 26
Croydon 19
Crystal Palace 78

Daft, Richard 26
Daily Express 82
Darling, Joe 39, 51, 66, 76
Derby 23, 30, 44
Derby (horse-race) 13
Derbyshire C.C.C. 23, 25, 29, 30, 43, 44
Derbyshire, Gentlemen of 44
de Trafford, C.E. 50
Docker, D. H. 44
Donald, Allan 99
Donnan, Henry 51
Dorking, Fifteen of 18
Doubtful Delivery Sub-Committee 26
Dowson, E.M, **79**
drought (1893) 24
Druce, N. F. **67**
Druce, W.G. 30
Dundonald Cricket Club 108

East, W.G. 120
Edgbaston 42
Education Act 1870 15
England 28-29, 35-41, 42, 49-57, 64-71
England cap **105**
Epsom Downs 13
Essex C.C.C. 12, 18, 22, 23, 24, 30, 31, 44, 59, 60, 72, 79, 82, 96, 105

Fairfield Recreation Ground 85
'Felix' 65, 69, 112
Fenner's 21, 30, 72
Findlay, W. 89
Flintoff, Andrew 37
Flowers, Wilfred 26
Forbes, D.H. 21
Forest Cricket Association (Nottingham) 22
Ford, F.G.J. **36**
Freeman, A.P. 45, 61, 124
Freeman, George 57, 119
Frith, David 8, 28, 35, 53, 96, 105, 132
Fry, C.B. 26, 42, 59, 76, 78, 80, 85
Fry, Philadelphia 8, 126
Fulford, Senator George T. 106
Fuller, Smith and Turner (brewery) 95

Gale, Fred 16
Gawlor 35
Gay, L.H. **36**
Geeson, Frederick 51
Gentlemen v Players 51, 59, 60, 89, 107
Giffen, George 28, 37, 40

Giggs Hill Green 48, 107
Gill, George 76
Gippsland 65
Glamorgan 16
Glasgow 94
Gloucestershire C.C.C. 22, 23, 27, 28, 30, 43, 55, 92, 102
Graburn, W.T. **32**, 78
Grace, E.M. 27
Grace, W.G. 7, 24, 27, 33, 45, 55,57, 75, 78, 89, 102
Grace Road, Leicester 28, 78
Graham, Henry 39, 51
Green, C.E. 120
Gregory, Syd 37, 38, 51, 57, 76
Guildford, Fifteen of 18
Gunn, William 29, 54, 55
gypsies 8, 13, 14

Hambledon 14
Hampshire C.C.C. 45, 51, 73, 77, 92
Hampton, Emma (see 'Cheesman')
Hancock's Cottages 9, **10**, 13
Harmsworth, St John 117, 118
Harry, John 39
Harvard (see Yale/Harvard)
Harvey, Tom 11, 16, **20**, **32**
Hastings 85
Hastings Festival 28, 45 , 61, 74
hat-tricks 27, 51, 73, 74, 125
Hayes, Ernest 74, 76, **79**
Hayward, Tom 42, 44, 47, 48, **50**, 54, 55, 58, 59, 60, 61, 62, **67**, 68, 70, 72, 75, **79**, 83, 85, 102
Headingley 37
Headlam, Cecil 77
Hearne, Jack 28, 51, 55, 59, 65, 66, **67**, 68, 70, 72
Henderson, Robert 24, 120
Higgs, Tom 18, 24, 119
Hill, Clem 66, 69
Hirst, George 28, 65, **67**, 68, 75, 83, 89
Hobbs, J.W. Club 19
Hobbs, Jack 7
Hodgsons' Kingston Brewery Cricket Club 83
Holland, Fred 42, **79**
Holmes, Rev R.S. 26, 40, 44, 46, 104
Howard, Ernest 120
Humphreys, W.A. **36**

ICC 12, 26
Iredale, Francis 39,40
Islanders, The 91

Jackson, F.S. 28, 55
Jardine, Douglas 44
Jephson, Digby 8, 21, **79**, 83
Jessop, Gilbert 75
Jones, Ernest 26, 49, 56, 58, 101, 102, 103

Keene, J. 16, **32**
Kelly, James 52, 76
Kent C.C.C. 30, 31, 43, 60
Key, Kingsmill 31, **50**, 51, 53

King, J.B. 61, 89
Kingston Cricket Club 85
Kingston Victoria Hospital 85
Knight, F. 120
Kipling, Rudyard 91
Kortright, Charles 23, 44

Laker, J.C. 125
La Corbière 110
Lancashire C.C.C. 24, 26, 27, 30, 33, 52,
    60, 62, 76, 86, 89
Larwood, Harold 22, 56
Lees, Peter 120
Lees, Walter 60, 61, 62, **79**, 120
lbw law 101, 125
Leicester 28
Leicestershire C.C.C. 18, 24, 28, 44, 50,
    58, 59, 73, 90
Leveson Gower, Sir Henry 21, 120
Leysse Gorge 110
Leyton 44, 59, 61, 78, 82
Lillee, Dennis 22, 56, 99
Lilley, Alan 52, 57
Lillywhite's 49, 99, 104, 105
Lindwall, Ray 99
linoleum factory 15, 19
Lizzie (flower seller) 120
Loader, Peter 124
Lock, Tony 124
Lockwood, Bill 21, 22, 24, 25, 27, 28,
    29,30, 31, **36**, 37, 38, 39, 40, 42,
    43, 47, 48, 49, **50**, 59, 73, 74, 75,
    76, **79**, 83, 86, 88, 89, 91, 99, 101.
    119, 124
Lohmann, George 7, 21, 22, 24, 25, 29,
    44, 46, 47, 49, **50**, 51, 52, 54, 55,
    58, 60, 61, 62, 66, 71, 82, 91, 99,
    101, 124, 125
London County 78, 85, 90
Longfellow, Henry 73
Lord's 31, 44, 49,51, 53, 54, 55, 59, 101
Luard, Arthur 27
Luton 19
Lyons, Jack 65
Lyttelton, Hon R.H. 101

McGahey, C.P. 79
McKibbin, T.R. 58
MacLaren A.C. **36**, 38, 39, 64, **67**, 68, 75
McLeod, Charlie 65
Marriott's XI 94
Marshall, Charles 42
MCC 56
Mason, Jack 65, **67**, 68, 69,
Melbourne 35, 38, 39, 40, 57, 65, 70
Melbourne Cricket Club 40, 41, 64
Melbourne Cup 70
Middlesex C.C.C. 30, 31, 53, 62, 86
Mitcham 9, 11, 13-20, 24, 57
Mitcham Common 10, 13
Mitcham Cricket Club 15, 16, **17**, 18, **19**,
    20, 21, 24, 48, 85, **90**, 91, 106, 119
Mitcham Fair 13, 14
Mitcham Green 11, **14**, 15, 16, **17**, **23**
Mitcham Wanderers 12, 16
Mold, Arthur 26, 28, 43, 58, 62, 101

Mollière (Les Molliennes) 113, 114, **116**
Montague, Eric 13, 14
Monte Carlo 107
Moreton-in-(the)-Marsh 22
Muller, Cyril 95
Murdoch, William 44, 45, 73

Nash, George 26
National School, Mitcham 14
New England, Twenty-two of 35
Newham, William 73
New Malden 88, 106
New South Wales 35, 70
New South Wales Cricket Association 40
New South Wales/Queensland XI 35
New York Times 89
Next XVII 50
Nicholas-Bar, Aix-les-Bains 108, **110**
Noble, Monty 92
North of England 28, 61
Northcliffe, Lord 117
Nottingham Forest 22
Nottinghamshire C.C.C. 19, 22, 25, 26,
    28, 29, 53, 78

Old Buffer's 12, 16
Old Trafford 6, 28, 52, 53, 54, 55, 104
Oval, The 12, 22, 24, 28, 30, 31, 42, 43,
    44, 50, 51, 53, 55, 59, 60, 62, 73, 74,
    75, 76, 78, 82, 83, 86, 89, 102, **103**,
    105, 107, 120
Owen, Hugh 79
Owers, A. 108
Owers, D. 108
Owers, F.G. 12, 108
Owers, J. 108
Oxford University 73, 86, 97
Oxford University Rugby XV 97
Oxford/Cambridge boat crew 82

Painter, John 30
Parr, George 41
Patel, Samit 105
Patterson, Alfred 95
Pearson, R. 16
Peel, Bobby 28, 35, **36**, 37, 40, 43, 45,
    46, 55
Perrier, Dr Louis 117
Perrier Water Company 117
personality 99-106
Philadelphia, Gentlemen of 89
Phillipson, E. **36**
Phipps Bridge, Mitcham 13, 14
pink pills 85, **87**, 97, 106
Platt, G. 120
Players 28
Poidevin, L.O.S. 91
Pougher, Arthur 42, 51
Powell, Col J. Leslie 120
Prince's Head, Richmond **95**, 96, 97,
    117, 118

Quaife, Walter 50
Queen's Head, Beddington Corner 11
Queensland 35

Radford 22
Ranjitsinhji, K.S. 21, 43, 52, 57, 59, 64, **67**, 68, 80, 85, 101, 108
Read, Maurice 22, 24, **29**, 48, **103**
Read, Walter 7, 11, 22, 33, 42, **50**
Recordine embrocation 85
Recreation Ground, Bath 6, 92
'Redskin Village' 13, 14
Reedman, John 37
Reigate Priory 33, 45
Rest of County (Somerset) 92
Rest of England 45
Rhodes, Wilfred 75, 78, 82, 83, 86
Richardson, Alice (sister) 9, 11, 126
Richardson, Bill (brother) 9, 11, 12, 120, 126
Richardson, Charles (brother) 9, 12, 15, 16, 108, 120, 126
Richardson, David John(great-great-nephew) 5, 12,128, 132
Richardson, Edith Emma (wife) 9, 95, 96, 97, 126
Richardson, Edith Norah (daughter) 11, 88, 96,126
Richardson, Elizabeth (Ellen) 9, 126
Richardson, Frank (brother) 5, 9, 12, 126, 127
Richardson, Harry (brother) 8, 9, 12, 15, 108, 119, 126
Richardson, Henry (father) 8, **9**, 126
Richardson, Johanna (née Bates) (mother) 8, **9**, 126
Richardson, John Henry (great-nephew) 127
Richardson, Kathleen (daughter) 11, 88, 96, 126
Richardson, Mary Lynn (great-niece) 132
Richardson, Matthew Frank (great-great-nephew) 127, 129
Richardson, Michael John(great-great-nephew) 127, 129
Richardson, Percival (Tubby)(nephew) 127
Richardson, Ralph Peter (great-great-nephew) 127, 129
Richardson, Rory James (great-great-nephew) 127, 129
Richardson, Terrence (great-great-nephew) 127, 129
Richardson, Tom passim
Richardson, Tom (son) 11, 88, 96, 108, 112, 126
Richmond cemetery 107, 119, **121**
Richmond Green 94, 95, 96, 109, 110, 113
Rockett, H. 120
Rose Cottage, Mitcham 13
Rotherham, H. 44
Rothermere, Lord 117
Royal Fusiliers 12
Royal United Hospital, Bath 92
Rugby Football Union 97
Rushby, Tom 120

St Jean d'Arvey 108, 110, 112, 113, 114
Scotland XI 94
Sharpe, John 21, 22, 48
Shaw, Alfred 22
Sheffield 28
Sheffield, Lord 40
Sheffield Shield 35, 68
Shrewsbury, Arthur 29, 78
Sinclair, Jimmy 82
Sissons, Ric 24
Smith, F.E. 30, 31, 43, **50**
Smith, G.O. 42
Smith, W.C. (Razor) 117, 120, 124, 125
Somerset C.C.C. 28, 30, 73, 74, 76, 86, 89, 92, 94
South Africa 5, 12, 21
South Africans 82, 90
South Australia 35, 38, 69
Southerton, James 15, 16, 125
Southampton 51
South of England 28, 61
Spofforth, Fred 103
Sporting Life 101, 105, 108, 113, 114, 116, 117, 118
Sporting Life fund 114, 117, **122**
star contract 47, 130
Statham, Brian 22
Stawell 35
Stedman, Fred **79**
Stoddart, A.E. 30, 35, 36, 38, 41, 47, 64, **67**, 69, 72, 75, 120
Stoddart's Anglo-Australian XI 45
Stoics Cricket Club 18, 81
Storer, William 65, **67**, 72, 75
Street, Alfred 42, **50**
strike 54
Strudwick, Herbert 15, 16, 88, 89 105, 106, 108, 119
Strutt-Cavell, William 97, 119
Stuckey, H. 66
Sugg, Frank 60
Sullivan, Dan 16
Surrey C.C.C. 18, 21-34, 42-48, 62, 72, 73, 74, 75, 76, 77, 82, 85, 86, 91, 102, 117, 118, 120, 123, 124, 125
Surrey Club and Ground 18
Surrey Colts 18
Surrey 2nd XI 19
Surrey & Sussex XI 75
Surrey Next XVII 50
Sussex C.C.C. 44, 45, 73, 74, 80, 82, 85, 97
Sydney 35, 37, 39, 64, 65, 66, 70

Taunton 30, 60, 74
technique 99-106
Thames Ditton 11, 19, 48
Thames Ditton and Surbiton Cottage Hospital 49
Thames Ditton Cricket Club **29**, 48, **63**, **81**, 85, 87, 107
Thomson, Jeff 22
Thornton, C.I. – England XI 72
throwing 26-27, 28, 79-80
Tonbridge Workhouse 8

Toowoomba 70
Toowoomba, Twenty-two of 35
Travers, Ben 77
Trent Bridge 25, 26, 29, 78, 80, 104
Trott, Albert 56
Trott, Harry 28, 51, 66
Trou des Enfers 114
Trueman, Fred 22, 56, 99
Trumble, Hugh 57, 76
Trumper, Victor 7, 76, 92
Tupling, Alfred Scott 91
Turner, C.T.B. 58
Turner, R. 16
Twain, Mark 108
Tyson, Frank 56, 99

Upminster Friars 12
Uppingham Rovers 44

Victoria, Queen 107
Victoria (state) 35, 66
Voce, Bill 22

Wainwright, Edward **67**, 68
Walker (groundsman, Trent Bridge) 26
Walker, Livingstone 88
Walsh, Courtney 22
Ward, Albert **36**, 40
Wardall, Thomas 28

Warner, Pelham 61
Warwickshire C.C.C. 29, 42-43, 50, 74, 75, 77
Wells, C.M. 42
Western Road, Mitcham 14
West Surrey Regiment, Queen's Royal 9, 12, 15
Whitgift Wanderers 19
Wilde, Simon 103
Williams, Dr. – pink pills 85, **87**, 97, 106
Willis, Bob 12
Winchester College 21
Wine Vaults, Bath 91, **93**
winter pay 31, 47, 86, 87, 88
Wisden 7, 25, 26, 31, 41, 45, 46, 54, 57, 61, 62, 66,75, 78, 85, 87, 91, 97, 100, 101, 104, 106, 107
Wood, H. **50**, 74, **79**, 120
Woodcock, Arthur 18
Woodrough (Ireland) 8
Woods, Sammy 92, 94, 101
Worcestershire C.C.C. 16
Wright, L.G. 25
Wyld, H.J. 86

Yale/Harvard boat crew 82
Yorkshire C.C.C. 25, 28, 30, 33, 43, 45, 53, 56,73, 74, 83